GEORGE H. MORRIS:
BECAUSE EVERY ROUND COUNTS

EDITED BY JOHN STRASSBURGER

A COLLECTION OF THE SHOW JUMPING LEGEND'S
50 BEST BETWEEN ROUNDS COLUMNS FROM
THE CHRONICLE OF THE HORSE
1989-2006

Trafford
PUBLISHING™

Photos front and rear cover, title page and section pages by Tricia Booker/
The Chronicle of the Horse. Photos in chapter 44 by Budd, Darling,
Marshall P. Hawkins and Foto-Mitschke

Note for Librarians: A cataloguing record for this book is available from Library and Archives
Canada at www.collectionscanada.ca/amicus/index-e.html
ISBN 1-4251-0264-6

*Printed in Victoria, BC, Canada. Printed on paper with minimum 30% recycled fibre.
Trafford's print shop runs on "green energy" from solar, wind and other environmentally-friendly
power sources.*

Offices in Canada, USA, Ireland and UK

Book sales for North America and international:
Trafford Publishing, 6E–2333 Government St.,
Victoria, BC V8T 4P4 CANADA
phone 250 383 6864 (toll-free 1 888 232 4444)
fax 250 383 6804; email to orders@trafford.com
Book sales in Europe:
Trafford Publishing (UK) Limited, 9 Park End Street, 2nd Floor
Oxford, UK OX1 1HH UNITED KINGDOM
phone +44 (0)1865 722 113 (local rate 0845 230 9601)
facsimile +44 (0)1865 722 868; info.uk@trafford.com
Order online at:
trafford.com/06-2021

10 9 8 7 6 5 4

Foreword

Every now and then, I have an idea that works, sometimes even one that *really* works. And that's what "Between Rounds" was.

In 1989, I was seeking to cement *The Chronicle of the Horse's* reputation for informed comment on the sports we cover, and I came up with the idea of asking a group of experts to write a column each month on the four disciplines that formed the bulk of each week's issue—hunters, jumpers, dressage and eventing. The big question was, who would those "experts" be?

I had no doubt about two of them, George Morris and Denny Emerson. Each had been—and still is—extremely influential and so very articulate. They each have an ability to challenge their students and anyone around them, to encourage them to ride better, to do more, to think beyond their present situation.

In hindsight, when they each said yes to my request, it guaranteed the success of Between Rounds, which would almost immediately become one of the magazine's most popular sections and the subject of more Letters to the Editor than any other section—a sure sign of the thought they've provoked.

For years, I've thought that someday I'd like to put together a book or books collecting the best thoughts of our columnists, and George gave me confidence in my idea when he called me one day in early 2005 and told me, in that signature baritone of his, "John, I think you should put together a book of my columns."

The question was, how? I didn't have time to do that and to put out a *Chronicle* each week. But then the stars fell into alignment when, in January 2006 I decided to retire from the *Chronicle* after 24 years. We then decided to expand George's suggestion into the "*Chronicle* Comment Series" of five books, collecting the best columns of George, Denny, Anne Gribbons and the late Victor Hugo-Vidal and adding a collection of my own Commentaries to the mix.

It also seemed logical to have George kick off the series since he is, well, a legend and an icon. I cannot think of anyone in the horse world whose name is more recognizable than his, thanks to almost 50 years of writing and teaching, quite literally, all around the world.

George Morris—the teacher and the man—is kind of a bridge between yesterday and today in horse sports. He's a bridge between the, frankly, elitist beliefs of the old U.S. Army crowd (men like Capt. Guy V. Henry and Brig. Gen. Harry Chamberlin), who believed that riding horses was an athletic endeavor that could be properly practiced only by those who devoted themselves to all aspects of it, and the populist outlook of Gordon Wright and Vladimir Littauer, who believed that nearly everyone could be taught to ride horses.

George studied the works of Henry, Chamberlin and others trained in the U.S. Cavalry, and he trained for years under Wright. He intrinsically believes that riding is a sport for which one must be physically prepared ("fit and thin," George would say) and that one must "do it right." But George helped foster, and has benefited greatly from, the dramatic expansion of all horse sports in the last 40 years, to an industry that Henry, Chamberlin (and even Wright) could never have imagined.

Only the rightfully sainted Bertalan de Nemethy has had a deeper and more thorough influence on riding in North America than has George. Before Bert, when George was a mere child, riding and particularly showing in the United States was a strange combination of seat of the pants and mystical. Few grasped or accepted the relationship between flatwork and jumping. Few understood—and none could explain—that a horse's acceptance and understanding of the rider's aids had a direct effect on how well that horse met the jumps and cleared them. Basically, you galloped at the jumps, and—unless you had "an eye" like Cappy Smith or Raymond Burr and could see the take-off spot from 30 strides away—you just hoped it worked out.

But Bert changed all that, forever, with his system of gymnastics based on measured distances. And in one of those cosmic coincidences, he was able to take under his wing a group of young men perfectly suited to performing under his system. George was one of them, along with Bill Steinkraus and Frank Chapot, and the four of them would revolutionize the way the world jumps horses over courses of fences.

In the following 50 columns, George explains his philosophy and vision in that clear and didactic style that's oh, so George. I decided to start with **What The USET Has Meant To Me For More Than 40 Years** and **A History Lesson** because they set the background of his philosophies about riding and of life. And the third chapter is, fittingly, his very first column, in which he describes **The American Style** that he helped shape.

Throughout, George will repeat similar themes as he foresees and analyzes numerous trends, events and situations. But that's because he believes repetition is the key to learning. And I think that you, like me, will find yourself saying, again and again, "George was right."

5

In looking back over the last 17 years, I'm proud of the impact our columnists have had on the horse world we cover. They've constructively criticized things that needed it and celebrated the things we've done well. And I believe that this collection, and the ones that will follow, will be something we'll all want to refer to regularly, to remind us of how things used to be or, at least, how they should be.

John Strassburger
September 2006

Introduction

The *Chronicle* has been a part of my life since the late 1940s, I suppose. I guess, like most hunter/jumper people, I always picked up and read it first thing when I got home from school or riding. It was a ritual—and still is.

First, I remember the paintings on the covers. Often, these paintings were of fabulous model horses; in those long-ago days, the conformation horses and the working hunter stars were the kings, the jumpers more of an afterthought. Now, the grand prix jumpers take centerstage.

Then, of course, I'd pore over every bit of news to be found in the "In The Country" section. It was my lifeblood. And we all read the horse show results scrupulously, line by line. Probably because all us juniors were in them and to check up on how our heroes were doing.

Remember, in those days, the *Chronicle* was the quickest means of accurate equestrian information and communication. We didn't have cell phones, email, fax machines, or the Internet. Nowadays, someone can be describing a round and the number of faults on a cell phone in Europe to an acquaintance in, perhaps, California. The result is known continents away before the class is actually pinned.

Not only have I always been a subscriber and avid reader of the *Chronicle*, but I have also been an advertiser. I have always believed in advertising, promoting and "getting the word out" through the means of this iconic paper. I have never been a great publicity seeker, and this weekly publication has done me just fine. I need not more.

To be perfectly frank, when John Strassburger asked me to write a monthly column called "Between Rounds" almost 20 years ago, I was quite surprised and deeply honored. I still am! Who would have thought as a teenager, star-struck by the *Chronicle*, that I would ever be a writer for this venerable paper? Certainly not me!

But the years went swiftly by (I honestly didn't know the exact number), and I realized I've written quite a few columns for the magazine. And so, a year or so ago, I asked John about the possibility of compiling these articles into a booklet of some sort—my compulsive, organizational nature at work. He thought about the idea, got back to me, and said it was a "go." I was delighted, of course.

People often comment to me about my writing, and I always respond to them the same way: I am not a writer, nor do I pretend to be one. I was never particularly trained in school to write, so I only write from passion on subjects that interest me.

The subjects I always tend to write about for the *Chronicle*, or anybody else, have to do with the history of equitation, theories of equitation, personal and practical truisms of equitation and horsemanship in general, veterinary practices, soundness, conformation, teaching riding, competitive riding, the U.S. Equestrian Team, and traveling with horses in mind.

John Strassburger has taken all these columns and divided them up judiciously into four categories. The first category has to do with the history and the evolution of horse sports. One of my favorite pastimes has been to indulge in horse literature, mostly how-to books. I attribute much of my success as a rider, trainer and teacher to my books. People today lose a lot of knowledge by *NOT READING!*

I have read historical how-to books from most, if not all, of the serious horse countries of the world. This gives me a great intellectual base from which to work when I mount a horse. It makes life much easier and infinitely quicker.

The second section is devoted to teachers and trainers. I was never the best rider, but I had the best teachers. They inspired me, yes, as a rider, but better still, to be a teacher, which I feel is my greatest contribution to the horse world. Over the years, I have tried, through my articles, clinics, or just teaching in general, to encourage other teachers "stay the course" when it comes to the classical principles and practices of correct equitation and horsemanship.

Following in the footsteps of the great Italian, French and American masters, I am a devoted disciple of the forward seat, and articles on this subject are the third section. I will stop at almost nothing to protect this ideology and its principles, positions and practices. I'm finding I have to work harder than ever to protect this method's sacred doctrines, which people are constantly trying to erase.

Articles on travel, clinics and USET interests make up the fourth section. Travel has always been a secondary passion of mine after horses, almost a compulsion. As a 2-year-old child having my first haircut, the barber saw that I had two crowns in my hair instead of one. He predicted to my father that I'd do a lot of traveling. Luckily, both these passions have intertwined, providing me with a life I was destined to have.

In the early 1950s, I traveled mostly in the Northeast on the national show circuit. I later traveled with the USET and Bert de Nemethy all over Europe on the international circuit. Then, I picked up wandering again with my clinics from the 1960s to the present. And now my job as chef d'equipe for the U.S. show jumpers takes me, mostly, to places I've been before, but also some new ones. I'm probably traveling more than ever.

I'm pleased to have all of this work put together in some cohesive way, if for no other reason than I can get to it easily as a reference. I cannot tell you how much I appreciate John's efforts in this respect. In turn, I can only hope it helps you readers with your own riding, traveling, and teaching. Perhaps, it will especially benefit the horses.

George H. Morris
September 2006

George H. Morris:
Because Every Round Counts

Table Of Contents

What Good Teachers Teach

I've Always Been Devoted To The Forward Seat

George, On Tour

14

It's Not Like It Used To Be

1

What The USET Has Meant To Me
For More Than 40 Years

January 6, 1995

I don't remember the last U.S. Army equestrian team of 1948, nor the catch-all 1949 team that included my teacher, Gordon Wright. I do, though, recall the "civilian" team of 1950, the first U.S. Equestrian Team.

It was memorable not only because its members weren't in the Army, but also because two of them were women. Carol Durand and Norma Mathews joined Arthur McCashin to form the squad. This was the first year I rode in the National Horse Show at New York's Madison Square Garden, and I was wide-eyed.

In 1951 Johnny Russell joined the team, and in 1952 Bill Steinkraus emerged riding the legendary Army horse Democrat. The New York papers ran headlines every day about Billy and Democrat because they won every individual class.

I got a bit of publicity on the weekend, when I won both the AHSA Medal and ASPCA Maclay finals on my good horse Game Cock. I was 14, and the double victory knocked me out of the

16

junior division prematurely. What was I to do, 14 years old and nowhere to go?

Gordon Wright suggested I go down the road to White Plains, N.Y., to Joe Verano, take some saddle seat lessons, and win the Good Hands and Saddle Seat medals. It wasn't a wild idea because in those days people often rode two or even three seats.

But my father wouldn't hear of it. He could only think of "the Team." So I decided at a very young age that my goal was to ride in the Olympics.

During the next few years, I rode on the USET at the fall shows with friends Charlie Dennehy and Ronnie Mutch. And that inspired me even more.

I always seemed to have lucky breaks or coincidences as a child. Victor Hugo-Vidal, another mentor, and I rode together at the Ox Ridge (Conn.) Hunt Club while growing up. He had a lovely young horse he decided to send to a new Hungarian trainer who had just arrived. Victor and I would go over to watch this man with the delicate touch ride his horse, who completely changed as the summer progressed. He relaxed, built up strength, and started to go like poetry in motion. This was, of course, Bert de Nemethy, years before he became the USET coach.

Another Hungarian literally awed the horse show community at the same time. He was an athlete and a superb horseman who wore white gloves. He'd longe and ride his horses only in snaffle bridles and did a lot of cavaletti work at the trot. He'd also trot down to very high fences.

In those days, we'd never seen such kind, quiet and sympathetic riding. Gabor Foltenyi, a friend of Bert's, trained in a new and difficult way and won many classes. Fortunately for me, he lived and showed on the East Coast, and I got to watch him by the hour.

17

A big year for the USET was 1955. As the story goes, McCashin, who had a good jumper named Matador, invited de Nemethy to visit him in New Jersey. Matador was supposed to be almost unrideable on the flat, but Bert asked to ride him. And the rest is history. Bert tamed the horse in 20 minutes and got the job.

I don't know if the story really is true. But I've heard it several times, and it sounds about right.

His first task was to field the 1956 Olympic team. We all trained that year in Tryon, N.C., under Bert. I'd never ridden under the structure and discipline of such flatwork, cavaletti and gymnastic jumping.

That spring, I really got hooked on the USET. Even though I had a great group of horses and a score good enough in the trials to put me on the team, my age and my total lack of European experience kept me off the team.

Although I was bitterly disappointed, nobody thought of a lawsuit. We just thought of the next time.

Bert wanted to stay home in 1957 to concentrate on young horses and riders and the national horse shows. It was the thrill of my life to be asked to go with him, Steinkraus, Chapot and Hugh Wiley to the summer shows. Being on the USET was the ultimate goal for any young jumper rider.

At the Piping Rock (N.Y.) Horse Show, Bert

"I'd like to see more people build their hopes, dreams and careers toward the long-term USET goals."

"The next three years were, possibly, the greatest years of my life."

18

announced to me that I didn't know how to "sit" and sent me to dressage trainer Richard Watjen, then in New York. Between Watjen, no stirrups and Mrs. Watjen standing in the corner, my seat improved before I returned to Tryon to report to Bert for a long training session before the European tour the next spring.

The next three years were, possibly, the greatest years of my life. Two passions of mine are horses and travel, and the USET combined both. It's hard to describe to young riders how educational and exciting it is to show all over the world, representing your country.

I finished fourth and rode on the silver-medal team in the 1960 Olympics. And at the ripe old age of 22, I decided my family had supported me enough and it was time to stand on my own and earn a living. I tried, unsuccessfully, to be an actor. So I decided to go back to horses, turn professional, and begin another passion—teaching. In those days you could not teach professionally and ride on the team as an international amateur.

I decided to teach with a mission—to produce riders who could ride on the USET and have the thrills I'd had.

Yes, the hunter and equitation divisions were terribly important to me all those years. And I wanted to learn to ride a hunter better. But my real thrill came when one of my students rode under de Nemethy, with Steinkraus and Chapot.

Today, though, many young people work hard toward short-term goals. I always knew the short-term goals (the Medal, Maclay or hunter championships) would happen if I trained people to think about long-term goals. The talent, money, energy, brains and other resources that go to these short-term goals are extraordinary. But too many talented youngsters drop out of sight, or "burn out," after a few years.

I'd like to see more people build their hopes, dreams and careers toward the long-term USET goals. No, it isn't easy, but it's possible.

The same applies to America's enthusiastic horse owners. Years ago, many of these people owned horses for our riders to show on the USET. Now, they're all riding at the horse shows. The level of instruction in this country has made this possible. It's a wonderful thing, to which I hope I've contributed.

I'm a great believer in the "trickle-down theory." We're only going to be as good as what represents us at the top. The higher the standard of success of our USET, the higher will be the standard of all our riding. It rubs off.

Let's get behind our elite riders. Support them a bit more, mount them better, send them abroad. Whatever makes a winning team and a winning country is what we should try to do, because there is a lot of talent out there.

2

A History Lesson

February 2, 1996

While we're busy patting ourselves on the back or criticizing ourselves to death, it can be instructive to compare the different areas of horse showing. I enjoy reviewing our history because I've been riding horses for about 50 years.

My earliest recollection of horses was during the early years of World War II. I grew up in New Canaan, Conn., a horsey suburb of New York City. Because of war shortages, our family had a victory garden and a cow (that I milked), even though my grandfather commuted to work on Wall Street every day. We also had a horse that we could ride or drive, and the gas rationing forced us to drive him all over town.

Fortunately for me, Margaret Cabell Self had her New Canaan Mounted Troop only a couple of miles away. My sisters had attended, my brother had attended, my father had been treasurer, and I was next in line. Mrs. Self's troop was also connected to the war effort. The whole country's mission was to win the war.

Once World War II was over, everyone's attention returned to the pursuit of leisure. I figure I'd had enough marching at troop and wanted more riding, so my family transferred me to the Ox Ridge Hunt Club in Darien, Conn. Otto Heuckeroth managed the club then, with an iron fist hidden in a velvet glove.

Otto was well ahead of his time and tried to teach us thickheads some basic dressage. I guess some of it rubbed off. Miss. V. Felicia Townsend was there and got many of us started in the right way. Our lessons were often out on the trails or in groups. Most of our ring work was done indoors in the winter. We rode bareback a lot too.

Most of the showing for the younger kids consisted of gymkhanas and club shows. They had all the fun classes you can imagine, which was great for our horsemanship. We used to ride to and from shows in Stamford and New Canaan because of the gas rationing.

The late '40s were a time when people were just getting themselves back in the ring and the hunting field. Everyone had been in a time warp.

When the 1950s rolled around, I was heavily into showing. I rode at the club with Otto and Miss T., and I started taking lessons with my great mentor, Gordon Wright.

Professionals then were usually men who had been grooms or apprentices for a trainer. They were real horsemen. Some had a flair for riding and became professional riders, but they were basically self-taught. A few men—like Gordon Wright, Raymond Burr, and Cappy Smith—had had formal training, either in the cavalry school at Ft. Riley, Kan., or from someone who'd been there, but they were the exception to the rule.

It was the same with the teachers. With the exception of Gordon Wright, Capt. Vladimir Littauer, Jane Dillon, Frank

Carroll, Al Homewood, Jimmy Williams and a few others, there were no teachers. And most of the good teachers were concentrated in the Northeast. The rest were good horsemen who taught people how to ride based on what they'd figured out for themselves.

Amateurs were usually wealthy people who really were amateurs. And all but a few really rode like amateurs. Peggy Augustus could regularly beat the pros. And Bill Steinkraus was technically an amateur for the sake of international participation, but he also was also the best rider in the country.

The hunters of the '40s and '50s still galloped and jumped. There were no three-foot sections, except in the early spring schooling shows. When a horse "came out" (the term we used for a green horse who hadn't shown recognized before) at Devon (Pa.) in May, he was expected to jump 3'6".

The courses were usually outside courses, long and up and down hill. The fences were solid and airy. Devon even had a wide ditch-and-log fence, as well as a table bank, on its outside course around the infield. The one-stride in-and-out was 31 feet, to be jumped in one stride. The working and conformation horses usually jumped 4'6".

The emphasis in those days was on pace. I'd say a hand gallop would be 14 to 16 miles per hour, and the open hunters often went more toward a racing gallop at 18 miles per hour. The good horses and riders had to have an eye at speed. A "miss" often meant a somersault.

Equitation was just another class, not really a division. Yes, there were equitation-minded juniors in those days. Many, including Bill Steinkraus and Victor Hugo-Vidal, showed in both saddle seat and hunter seat, something unheard of today. Yes, winning the AHSA Medal, ASPCA Maclay or a championship was

23

important. But riding your horse in different classes was more important.

Until the mid-'50s, equitation courses were very simplistic: post-and-rail fences, twice around the outside, or side-diagonal-side. During the '50s, the courses changed drastically.

The jumper division was for horses who couldn't make hunters. It was the stepchild division, and the performances often looked like a circus. Characters like Joe Green, Johnny Bell, Harry de Leyer, George Braun and Al Fiore were great riders and would perform like actors on a stage. It was part of the show. Bill Steinkraus, Raymond Burr, Cappy Smith and Gabor Foltenyi were ahead of their time because they showed jumpers with elegance and style.

The jumper courses in the '50s were also terribly simplistic. The fences were mostly single rails or railroad gates. The spreads were triple bars, with few combinations. Most of the classes were rubs (touches to count) or knockdown-and-out. Occasionally there was a class under FEI rules, but it was nothing like the real thing in Europe.

The 1960s were radical for our society and the horse community. It was a decade that took the hunters and jumpers from the dark ages into the modern, technological era of horsemanship. This would prove both good and bad, and there were logical reasons for the transition at this time.

Gordon Wright was the undisputed No. 1 teacher in the country after the war. He was an extraordinarily gifted communicator and psychologist, and a great horseman. Gordon was a boy from New York who in his youth found his way West to try his hand at being a cowboy. He returned to the East in 1927 to compete in the rodeo at the old Madison Square Garden in New York City. He decided that a career riding broncs was more than a bit risky, so he took his prize money and opened his first riding school in Westchester County, N.Y.

He developed a nice hunter/jumper clientele during the '30s and took lessons once a week from Co. "Gyp" Wofford at West Point. Gordon then enlisted at Ft. Riley during the war, and that's where he really became educated.

During the '60s, Gordon Wright's first post-war generation of riders started to turn professional: Victor Hugo-Vidal, Ronnie Mutch, Wayne Carroll and me. For the first time, his system of educated riding was spreading to the masses. Before that, knowledge was mostly confined to a few metropolitan areas— New York, Detroit, Chicago, Houston, and Los Angeles. Jimmy Williams, another cavalry officer, contributed an enormous amount to people on the West Coast, producing Marcia "Mousy" Williams, Robert Ridland, Susie Hutchison, Hap Hansen, Rob Gage and Ronnie Freeman. Now these people began to teach.

Bert de Nemethy captained perhaps the greatest and most consistent, and certainly the most stylish, team the world had seen at the time. His system started to creep out from the ivory tower at Gladstone, N.J., and spread. He taught us cavaletti, gymnastics and related distances. We, in turn, taught others.

With this turn toward precision, the amateur could no longer really compete with the professional. So the amateur-owner hunter

"The hunters of the '40s and '50s still galloped and jumped."

"The 1960s were the pinnacle decade for the American hunter."

25

division came into being. It gave the amateurs a place to show and gave the pros a chance to sell horses that couldn't jump 4 feet.

Bert de Nemethy was also a gentleman and a charmer. He gave professionalism, jumper riding and the USET a class and status they never had before. It was unheard of before this time for a "lady" or a "gentleman" to think of becoming a professional horseman. Without even knowing it, Bert gave the professional horseman credentials, sort of a college degree.

There were probably more philanthropic owners during that decade than ever before. Owners such as John Galvin, Eleo Sears, Theo Randolph, Patrick Butler, Whitney Stone, Jessie Cox and Walter Devereaux were lining up to donate horses to the USET, mainly because of Bert's management and training methods. Bert received the horses and matched them with one of his riders. He also had access to any young rider in the country. Winning the Medal or Maclay was so important because it caught Bert's eye.

Courses changed dramatically in the '60s. Hunter classes started to "pull in" from the long, permanent courses, and the equitation and jumper courses started to look more international. This was largely because of the influence of two people—Dr. Robert Rost and Pamela Caruthers. She had such a great influence on courses, horses and riders by getting us going forward.

Our horsemanship had more or less caught up with the rest of the world, we still had access to nearly unlimited numbers of big Thoroughbred horses, the USET was at the top of its game, and the equitation division was turning out rider after rider with Olympic potential. From the mid-'60s until the early '80s, we were the best, the envy of the world.

Benny O'Meara, a Brooklynite like me, became a legend in his own time for a few short years before his tragic death in his own souped-up airplane in April 1966. Benny showed us another way to ride and win. With his legs out on the dashboard, his seat in the back of the saddle, and his hands under his chin, Benny would canter into any ring and win.

While his style and de Nemethy's were totally opposite, for some reason they complemented each other and got along well. Benny and Kathy Kusner produced many great horses for the team, and Kathy also became her own living legend. I believe that if Benny had lived, he would have modified his style considerably.

Benny influenced many people, including a young star who was rising fast—Rodney Jenkins. Rodney learned from everybody, but especially from his father, Ennis, and from Bobby Burke and Benny. Rodney will probably be our horseman of the century. There is nothing he can't do, hasn't done, or doesn't know about horses.

For 30 years, Rodney epitomized the American style of riding and horsemanship. The whole world has tried to copy parts or all of it. Rodney distilled the old Virginia hunting seat, Benny O'Meara, Bert de Nemethy, hunter seat equitation and European methods, put it all together, and made it work. Some people try to copy his idiosyncrasies and mannerisms, but they can't.

Rodney's archrival was Bernie Traurig, the jewel of Littauer's crown, a winner of both the Medal and Maclay. Bernie was and still is a classicist and stylist of the highest order. He and Rodney ran head-to-head with the hunters and the jumpers for years and years. Primarily because of these two men, and because of Katie Monahan Prudent, the 1960s were the pinnacle decade for the American hunter.

Hunter riding still had the individuality, freedom and brilliance of the earlier years, coupled with the precision and technique of modern showing. And when these individuals left the hunter arena, the lights dimmed a bit.

The 1970s, and even well into the 1980s, were the years of our victories. They were the fruits of the labor of so many native and naturalized American horsemen for so many years before.

Bert de Nemethy retired in 1980, and many of the older generation of really great horsemen—Dave Kelly, Adolph Mogavero, Bob Freels, Bobby Egan—also retired or died. Others who were still going strong shifted to other pursuits. Voids were left on many different fronts, but we couldn't do much about it.

Frank Chapot carried on brilliantly for Bert: The team gold and individual gold and silver medals at the 1984 Olympics, team gold and individual silver at the 1986 World Championships, silver team and individual medals at the 1988 Olympics, individual bronze medal at the 1992 Olympics, and seven FEI World Cup Final victories from 1979 to 1987.

But it's a different society today. Since the late '80s, the values of this society are being reflected in our own sport. Everything revolves around money. It's a vicious cycle. *Money is the root of all evil.* The values in the horse business aren't there anymore.

Where has class gone? Where have standards, dress and behavior gone? One has to go abroad to find real work ethic and real discipline.

Teaching today is very different than 30 years ago. People think they work hard and have self-discipline. Most do not, unfortunately. We live in a soft, self-indulgent, weak society. I'm talking about moral fiber and the ability to suffer mental and physical discomfort.

We've had it too easy in America. The same thing is happening in Europe, but they're about 10 years behind us.

The '80s and '90s have given us professional horsemen who micromanage. They're often quite good at their specialty, but few have great range as horsemen. Few will ever be remembered as giants in their field. Yes, a lot of them ride well, but is that enough to carry over to the future generations?

How many of today's amateur-owners are really amateurs? Lots of ribbon winners in these divisions aren't amateurs. Everything has gotten too expensive. Even honest people are cheating.

Where are the philanthropic owners of old? Yes, there are some out there. Usually, though, they have selfish motives at heart. Rarely do they give for the sake of the sport. That's why the open hunter divisions, the grand prix classes and the USET are all limping a bit. The owners of old were people passionate for the "sport of kings."

One of the problems with today's hunters is that the jumper division has eclipsed their glamour. There isn't any "blood and guts" in the hunter division any more. People want that feeling in the pit of their stomach once in a while. It's too soft, easy and boring now. It's headed in this direction in the jumper division too.

The hunter seat equitation division can be no better or worse than the standard in the hunter division. These two divisions are inseparably intertwined, as they should be. We always took our top horses and riders from the hunter ring to the equitation ring, to the jumper ring, and then to the team. That was our American recipe for success. That's why we produced so many top international horses and riders.

It's the hunter professionals' and the show managers' job to get off their backsides, be inventive, and put some sport and theater back into the hunter and equitation divisions. I can't understand this apathy. Showing in this country, for the most part, is like being part of a dysfunctional family.

This is just a glimpse of my six decades of going to horse shows in the United States. I'm sorry I can't be more positive,

29

but it's like training a spoiled horse or teaching an uneducated rider—there's work to be done and something to create. Without creativity and improvement, life would be a bore.

This horse business must have something, though. I'm jumping into my car to go to yet another show a little farther away than the New Canaan Mounted Troop. This one is in West Palm Beach, Fla.

Yes, we horse people are probably all a bit nuts.

3

The American Style

July 7, 1989

At the Rome International Horse Show, I watched the American team of Joe Fargis, Katie Prudent, Beezie Patton [Madden] and Debbie Dolan [Sweeney] in the Nations Cup and rode myself as an individual. What struck me so there is the American style, which the world is eager today to copy.

Who wouldn't want it? The "look" is unique and so, so classy. How does one define this style or explain it? Like everything else, it is a question of infinite detail and can be broken down and explained. To copy it would be next to impossible, though, unless one lived in America and really absorbed it. Yes, we can export bits and pieces, but not the whole item intact.

Taste and class involve simplicity, beauty and cleanliness. Yes, cleanliness, my fellow horsemen, *is* next to godliness! Believe me, just go and travel.

At home or at a show, this begins with the physical facility. At the horse show we call it the "set-up." In Rome, the U.S.

Equestrian Team set-up had the right look—very simple, scrupulously clean and therefore beautiful.

I first became aware of top-class stable management traveling abroad with Bert de Nemethy and Bob Freels. The USET always did it right, not overdone with landscaping surrounding an antique shop. I don't believe in anything flashy or artificial, especially connected with horses.

In Rome, all the equipment was neat and orderly, as it should be—a simple stable banner, tack trunks in place and perfectly stacked, stalls clean and banked, two water buckets, blanket racks, junk stalls, and even the garbage organized.

Riders, trainers, grooms and managers were always doing something—working. Whether it was writing out a work list, picking out a stall, cleaning tack, or washing a horse, the wonderful American work ethic was present. And all of this before and after the fact of riding, schooling and showing. In other words, stable management is the *sine qua non* of the American style.

What foreigners do not realize is that our good horsekeeping precedes everything else we might do well. This is where it's at; this is our secret.

Watching our riders walk out to work on the flat or to school their horses lightly before the show did my heart good. The extension of Ft. Riley (Maj. Harry D. Chamberlin, Gordon Wright and Bill Steinkraus), coupled with de Nemethy's tremendous influence of cavaletti and gymnastic work, was so apparent.

Very few horsemen do this part so well—beautiful position, soft use of aids, and a myriad of flatwork exercises. The way our riders prepare themselves and their horses is so natural and simple, therefore the beauty. Whether it be the ball of the foot on the stirrup, the upper body with the movement of the horse (and not behind it!), smooth transitions, or the long/short release, it is a pleasure to watch.

Needless to say, all of this hard work, detail and philosophy carry over into the ring. If any part of this intricate preparation (for us a normal procedure) were missing, it would seriously change our performance and, therefore, the American style the world sees.

There is no quick fix, no recipe that can make it work during a competition. As we Americans all know, it has been years, decades and generations in the making. It's hard to explain, let alone teach, to friends around the world that this "style thing" is a reflection of our way of life with horses.

It certainly can't be exported, nor can it be bought. Fortunately, it stands out in world competition and is most definitely ours to keep.

"I don't believe in anything flashy or artificial, especially connected with horses."

"It stands out in world competition and is most definitely ours to keep."

4

The Indoor Shows: More Of The Same

December 1, 1989

The indoor shows have come and gone again, more quickly than ever it seems. In relation to all the other good horse shows the rest of the year, they not only go by in a blink, but they also are not all that important.

Yes, the AHSA Medal and ASPCA Maclay Finals are *the* finals, but the other classes, division championships, and even the grand prix (except that they are World Cup-qualifying classes) are not much different anymore than what's offered the rest of the year.

Years ago, winning indoors was something so special, so different. Now, to me, it blends in much more with the A-rated shows and grand prix events the whole year long.

We never showed nearly so much, the year was much shorter, rubbing shoulders with foreign riders was quite unusual, grand prix classes like the President's Cup (Washington, D.C.) were so special, and now all that has changed. This wall-to-wall, back-to-back, week-to-week showing is the name of the game and a sign of our modern society.

Yes, some things are infinitely better—the scientific approach to riding and training, for instance. However, some things are appallingly worse—namely the sometimes-total disregard for horse or pony!

Baltimore, ever since the World Cup Finals held there in 1980, has always had tremendous potential. And I'd still say the same. Baltimore has the potential, but nothing has ever happened. This city is in the very heart of an enormous horse community. Not only the "horsey" state of Maryland, but also Virginia, Pennsylvania, Delaware, New Jersey and Washington, D.C., are all right there. What a built-in audience if someone cared enough and knew enough to tap it and get the people there.

Being a jumper show, it's imperative that there be an atmosphere. To create an atmosphere, one needs an audience. But even some of the residents of the hotel across the street didn't know a horse show was going on. To add insult to injury, there were literally thousands of people (mostly tourists) milling about throughout the lovely October weekend along the Inner Harbor with nothing to do. I'm sure many of them would have loved to be entertained by a well-done show jumping event coordinated with an exciting exhibition or two.

From our point of view, the show couldn't have gone better: Good stabling, excellent footing, imaginative fences and courses by Steve Stephens, plenty of time to work in the mornings.

Two things, though, really did irk the exhibitors: 1) The extremely long hours mostly devoted to wasted space in between classes with nothing going on; and 2) The $100 entrance charge to a nice little sandwich-and-drink bar. In other countries, not only are the ringside bars and restaurants usually deluxe, but also the riders, trainers and owners are invited repeatedly to come and enjoy—for free! Let's face it, haven't we all, the aforementioned, paid our dues just getting to the show?

Harrisburg (Pennsylvania National) has always, and I mean for decades, been a horse show I've liked. It's a wonderful show grounds for the horse, the trainer and the rider—a horseman's horse show. The stabling is the best, the outdoor schooling area most ample, and the indoor arena the finest in which to ride anywhere. This year the footing was excellent, back to what it used to be before they tampered with it a few years back.

What has deteriorated over the years most is the maintenance. This used to be a very clean building, and Harrisburg and the show itself were really elegant. The locals used to dress to the nines and pack the house every night. Now the crowds flock to the grand prix and perhaps to support another night or two really well. With just a little sprucing up, house cleaning, and more promotion, the show could return to what it was in the '50s, when the international teams rode there.

Washington also has a marvelous complex at the Capital Centre in Landover, Md., surrounded by an historic horse community, a stone's throw from the nation's capital. The outdoor stabling is fine, as long as Mother Nature cooperates just a little bit. Usually at this time of year that's not a problem. The stabling area does get a bit used and dirty, mostly because this show is too long—eight days. Couldn't they tighten this show up a bit?

It's more than the number of days; the hours have become too extreme too. The grooms are awake more or less around the clock for the week, and so is everyone else. The schooling sessions have to start way before dawn because many days the show begins at 7 or 7:30 a.m.! By the time a jumper has been wrapped and properly put to bed, it's often midnight.

The first rule of good theater is to pick up the pace and cut things down. Don't bore! There are too many extraneous exhibitions, acts, friends and family of directors, and horses in that ring as part of the show. If this were all tightened considerably, it could be one of the best in the world.

The new footing this year was abrasive and hard and made horses sore. Unfortunately, it wasn't much better than in previous years. While showing and working a horse here is quite good, the shopping arcade and restaurant are first rate.

The Meadowlands is an excellent show facility for the National Horse Show. It is an important show. No, it is not Madison Square Garden; it's not in New York City and never will be. One cannot compare the two; it's really unfair to try. They aren't even in the same state.

Getting to the wonderful Meadowlands Arena complex is fairly easy if you can just read and follow directions. And a magnificent complex it is—clean, spacious and staffed by in-house people.

Some of the amenities are: huge parking areas safely fenced in; room for stabling that could be improved with larger tents; the covered outdoor August A. Busch Jr. Memorial Pavilion for showing, schooling and exercising; food trucks; several good restaurants; an arcade much like Washington; good footing; and a large, galloping ring. Tradition, atmosphere and a cozy ambiance are missing, but they should come in time.

All in all, though, one must admire this show's first attempt and admit this is a good horse show, even though most of us miss The Garden terribly. Times, unfortunately, change, and that's simply a fact of life.

The feeling at The Meadowlands is an extension of Washington and not the electric climax of Broadway and New York, and that has really put these indoor shows into perspective. They certainly aren't the be-all and end-all they used to be. Rather, the indoor circuit is another five weeks of very good showing.

Yes, people will still very much want to qualify, although not quite so desperately as before. They will occasionally elect to go to some other good circuits during other times of the year. Madison Square Garden in the "Big Apple" was quite a pot of gold at the end of a very long rainbow.

I hope we're developing horsemen and horsewomen enough to see that there are other goals in life besides getting points for indoors.

5

The Balance of Power Is Shifting

June 1, 1990

For years, North America tried to reign supreme as a show jumping power. But it wasn't until the 1980s that our continent was the one to beat as far as jumping was concerned.

World Cup after World Cup (10 to be exact) was ours for the taking, the victor being either an American or a Canadian. We even captured the team gold and individual gold and silver at the Olympics in 1984, the team gold and individual silver at the World Championships in 1986, and an additional double silver at the Olympics in 1988. It appeared as though nobody could come close.

The tide finally turned this year in Dortmund, West Germany, at April's FEI World Cup Final. Just by the law of averages the Europeans had to win. They were long overdue. Granted, they had the strongest team they could muster, and we didn't because some of our top riders and horses stayed home preparing for the World Championships in July.

I was actually very proud of the young riders, greener horses and new combinations we did send. To have four in the top 10 still isn't bad. It's really very good.

Bernie Traurig, on Maybe Forever, was the only rider to achieve a double-clear round on the last day, and he did it in a style and manner that few can ever achieve. He gave the world yet another classic American riding lesson and finished eighth.

Michael Dorman and Chris Kappler finished seventh and ninth. They rode beautifully and most consistently over very difficult courses. Beezie Patton [Madden] and Gusty Monroe, a new partnership, had some effortless trips to end up 10th.

Talk about riding lessons! Watch Beezie ride championship courses. For that matter, watch her do anything on a horse.

Why then, with our wonderful riders and teachers, are we going to see the power balance lean back toward the Europeans?

The first reason is technical. The Europeans lagged behind us for quite a long time, "knowing" they were better. Suddenly they weren't. Not only was our stable management and veterinary care way ahead of theirs (it had been for decades), but suddenly our riding positions, flatwork, gymnastics and ability to read lines and courses were also better.

There wasn't much they could do with a show jumper that we couldn't do better. Our horses came to the ring very sound and in beautiful condition. They rode well due to our more natural, lighter approach to dressage work. Our positions on horseback were definitely more stable due to our equitation and hunter training. And, thanks to Bert de Nemethy, we were brought up on a variety of gymnastics and striding.

Now, my friends, to a great extent they have caught up on many, if not all fronts. What really impressed me was the German Equitation Finals at Dortmund. Thirty juniors rivaled our Medal/

Maclay competitors. Not only was their style on a par with ours, but they also angled fences, trotted a bounce, made canter-trot-canter transitions on course, rode broken lines, changed horses, and jumped a bit higher and wider.

Nonetheless, I doubt that the masses in Germany or the rest of Europe will ever really catch up to us, let alone surpass us technically. They just don't think the way we do, which is to our advantage. It's the next point that's more difficult to combat.

Experience. Yes, our top riders in North America have the technical ability, the mental attitude, and the "mileage around the block" to ride head and head with anyone in the world. The rest of us are lacking in experiencing the variety of pressures that Europeans find every weekend.

By experience I mean riding in different countries, under varied conditions, over strange fences, against a constantly changing number of competitors, in various classes.

The most important classes are the Nations Cups. Working together as a team at shows all season long and producing under that special pressure of a Nations Cup is something for which there is no substitute. Practice by doing it is the only way, but it's hard for us to compete a lot in Nations Cups because of where we live.

Despite this handicap, we have proven over the years that, due to our fabulous standard and

"The Europeans lagged behind us for quite a long time, 'knowing' they were better."

"What then is my biggest fear? Horseflesh!"

41

preparation at home, we can do it when the moment counts.

What then is my biggest fear? Horseflesh!

I've said it before, and I'll say it again: We (and I include myself at the top of the list) have painted ourselves into a corner. We've allowed our internal market to die. Where are our North American Thoroughbreds of yesteryear? Where are all our horse dealers of old? And where are all the good horsemen making young jumpers?

Thanks goodness for the new International Hunter Futurity and the even newer International Jumper Futurity. They may well help to save the day. We need to be able to have our own great young prospects available here at home for us. Between the fabulous prize money, automobiles, prestige, medals and rich owners and sponsors, the Europeans would be fools to sell us their best horses or even prospects. And, believe me, they aren't fools.

A top horse in Europe now either slips away by blind luck or one pays through the nose. More often, top horses simply aren't for sale.

We are the best riders, but there are lots of wonderful riders today all over the world. Remember the bottom line: It's a horse-jumping contest.

To have the best, we need to breed them, find them, make them, and market them. Let's not forget Gem Twist, Pressurized, Albany, For The Moment, Touch Of Class, Jet Run, Kahlua, and all the other North American Thoroughbred and Thoroughbred-type horses we've had.

Charity begins at home, and it's foolish and risky to believe that other people in other lands will provide us with rides to beat them at their own game, the game they love most—international show jumping.

6

Just One More Jump!

April 5, 1991

When I was growing up, the good horsemen of old taught me one of the most important lessons in good horsemanship: A horse has just so many jumps in him, no more. For every fence you take, there is one less at the other end.

The English, perhaps the best horseman of all, also feel this to be true. They also have another great saying: "One runs out of horse the day before one runs out of horse shows."

Michael Matz, Joe Fargis and Frank Chapot know these truths, but 90 percent of the young horsemen in this country today do not. I can always tell by the way people school and show their horses. The really great trainers and riders don't jump much. They know better.

Nowadays, I know the problem is qualifying. This is true all over the world, not just in the United States. There are just so many good horses and riders everywhere, be they hunters, jumpers or equitation riders.

The trick is to be a clever trainer and try to save the jumps for the ring. Don't waste a lot of beautiful, expressive jumping efforts outside the ring. Don't lose the class at home or in the schooling ring. If a rider is a novice or has a limited ability, he must have a school or practice horse. He simply cannot benefit himself by using up his good horses. I will not allow it.

Everybody, and I mean everybody, agrees that hunters today are not the same. Most of us know exactly what happened to the hunters. While the mechanics, the perfection, the dressage are there, the expression, the enthusiasm and the athleticism are not.

When I ride and judge hunters, the one thing I really care about is a good jumper. Playing on the end of the ring is not the end of the world (although cross-cantering is); a mediocre mover, while not good, is not usually life-threatening. I don't look for a high- or low-headed horse or a swishy tailed, ear-pinning, sour type, but if the beast can jump, so be it. At least I'll get to the other side.

Today in our hunter world, we are seeing mostly "steppers," not jumpers. And most people know it. Through the excessive longeing, drilling and practice jumping, the horses no longer care or are sound enough to jump up. They simply step.

There is nothing more alarming (at worst) or more boring (at best) than a steppy jumper.

44

It means he is either sore or bored, or probably both. Those of you who have jumped these horses know that it can be just plain dangerous.

In the jumper world, fortunately, the practice jumping and drilling usually backfire. The horses get a bit sore, short-strided, bored and dull. They jumped lower, lose a bit of scope, and start hitting the fences. There is no cleaner jumper than a fresh, sound horse who wants to put out simply because he feels good and is impressed, not because he's been hammered at.

So the best trainers and riders, those who keep away from the jumps, usually get their just rewards in the jumper ring.

The problem that jumpers are facing worldwide is forced jumping. The qualifying, money-won and computer rankings in today's world to even get to the end-of-the-year shows, let alone the FEI World Cup Finals or international teams, probably force even the best horses to show too much.

I know that the average good horse has to show too much. As far as I'm concerned, 15 to 20 shows per year for our nice grand prix horses is more than enough. For a great, great horse like Gem Twist, 10 shows a year would be more like it.

I'm talking about people who want to keep a nice horse around for awhile, say eight, 10 or 12 years. Most of the good horses today disappear after three to five years. But they're too hard to find and replace to lose so quickly.

What worries me when considering our representation internationally is that we have enough fresh, sound championship horses at our disposal when the time comes. Looking back over the past, I doubt very much whether our best Olympic and World Championship horses could have stood the gaff of today's showing demands.

Horses like Calypso, Albany, Livius, Touch Of Class, Jet Run, Silver Exchange, Sandsablaze, Bonte II, Sloopy, San Lucas, Snowbound, Ksar d'Esprit, Riviera Wonder and Sinjon. If they had stayed sound while being over-shown, would they have been as good?

We all know that to win one of those special days, our horses must be very, very good. If we've gone to the well too often, I'm afraid there won't be enough left to drink.

Time will tell. We have a hard act to follow in producing international show jumpers: Bert de Nemethy's legacy of the past 35 years.

7

And The Gap Widens...

May 10, 1991

To me, any horse show has always been a test indicative of where horse and rider stand relative to the competition. Whether it's a pre-green horse at a local show, a Maclay finalist, or an Olympic horse, it makes no difference. It's still just a test of where you are in comparison to the others.

The FEI World Cup Final, on a yearly basis, provides a wonderful opportunity for us North Americans to realistically see where we stand in relation to the rest of the world, primarily the Europeans.

Last month at the World Cup Final in Gothenburg, Sweden, the truth came out. With the exception of Anne Kursinski and Debbie Shaffner, who tied for seventh, we had no others in the top 10. Yes, we did have some young riders and horses who went well. But our showing was a far cry from that of just a few short years ago, when we consistently dominated this championship.

What is going wrong, and is it fixable? I believe we have serious problems that will not be easy to remedy.

The first problem is too much democracy, which always causes a malady called "too many chiefs and not enough Indians." We all know in our hearts this is going on now in our American horse community. No good comes of it.

Discipline, structure, system and excellence always suffer as a result.

Just the opposite is true in the show jumping powers of Europe—England, France, Germany and Holland. There are clearly chiefs and clearly Indians. More gets done better that way.

Of course, the disgusting American pastime of litigation doesn't help. It just weakens the whole. People around the world are watching and scratching their heads in amazement.

How we have defeated ourselves! We've come a long way down, my friends, since the era of Bert de Nemethy, an era stamped with dignity and class.

Problem No. 2 has to do with experience, international experience. Experience is "doing." Even our elite riders must, from time to time, experience competition abroad.

The shows abroad are different, the classes are different, the other competitors are different. No matter how tough the courses and competition are at home, it's just not the same as at a big international show.

And the overall standard of competition in Europe is so much better than 10 years ago. They've learned all of our "strokes" well, and we've not kept up or learned any of theirs.

Problem No. 3 is horseflesh. Yes, our American Thoroughbred is probably the best in the world. But we can't get to all the good Thoroughbreds. They are bred for the track, and they go there. If we had easy access to all the good blood horses in our country, it could be a different story. But we don't.

The Europeans have traditional, sophisticated and detailed programs for the breeding and development of jumping horses. We're just starting to do that.

At the same time, most of our good old American horse dealers have become extinct. We don't have dealers the way we used to, and that's too bad. They always had an ample supply of prospects.

"In the show jumping powers of Europe, there are clearly chiefs and clearly Indians."

Everyone in Europe deals, so there's an endless number of sport horses to see. It's not that we don't have the time or the shows to make our jumpers. We just don't have enough of the right types available at the start.

Let's be honest with ourselves. We do not reign supreme in show jumping like we did. If we want to remain in contention at the Olympics, World Championships and the World Cup, we've got to pull ourselves together internally.

We have to demand our show managers provide simulated international show jumping conditions, look for ways to compete abroad, and find and develop Olympic-type horses in North America.

"Let's be honest. We do not reign supreme in show jumping like we did."

Nobody else is going to do it for us. With the World Cup Final coming to Del Mar (Calif.) next April and Atlanta hosting the Olympic Games in 1996, there is pressure on us to produce. That pressure will be good for our sport.

8

Bill Steinkraus—The USET's Role Model

February 28, 1992

In this age of coup d'etat and hostile takeovers, it's especially important for our young horsemen to remember where they came from and who was responsible for getting them where they are today. It's good for some our older horsemen to remember this too, because many seem to have forgotten.

We've been lucky to have had some great riders and teachers since the war—and I mean World War II, not Desert Storm. We couldn't have done without brilliant trainers like Bert de Nemethy, Jack Le Goff, Gordon Wright, Vladimir Littauer and Jimmy Williams. A role model competitor is something different, however. He or show is in the ring at the top level of competition, winning classes. Nothing less will really influence an entire nation.

Many countries have had great riders and leaders in the last 40 years. The Germans had Alwin Schockemohle, a great horseman and Olympic winner in 1976, but by no means a stylist. The French had Pierre Jonqueres d'Oriola, who wasn't a great technician by any means but was an intuitive gallop-and-jump rider who nobody could copy and who twice won Olympic gold medals. The British produced Pat Smythe and Harry Llewelyn, who, while great winners, rode by the seat of their pants in the old-fashioned way. And the Italians did have Piero and Raimondo d'Inzeo, two great stylists who evidently weren't able to pass on what they knew to the masses.

"A consummate stylist who, by his example of class on horseback, would influence American riders, teachers and trainers for generations."

But we have had a consummate stylist who, by example of class on horseback, would influence American riders, teachers and trainers of all disciplines for generations. That man is Bill Steinkraus.

Billy and I had similar backgrounds growing up. We were each from ultraconservative families who, although supportive of horses, didn't hand out much on a silver platter. We both grew up in and around Fairfield County, in southern Connecticut. He started with Ada Thompson in Wilton and I with V. Felicia Townsend at the Ox Ridge Hunt Club in Darien. Both were wonderfully gentle but firm horsewomen from the English school who gave us a perfect start.

"Nobody in our lifetime will ever equal Bill Steinkraus as an all-around horseman."

Although Billy is about 10 years older than I am, we each rode with the legendary Gordon Wright and later together on the U.S. Equestrian Team with Bert de Nemethy.

Billy was everybody's role model in the early '50s, and his influence only increased as he rode in five Olympic Games between 1952 and 1972,

51

winning the individual gold medal in 1968. He was one of the few who could ride hunters and jumpers equally well and win in a beautiful style. He was a horseman's horseman, so both he and his horses were always turned out perfectly.

The kids of that era all wanted to ride like Bill Steinkraus. All of today's American riders and teachers can directly or indirectly trace their methodology back to him.

As a junior, I can well remember watching Billy from afar. He would come to the Ox Ridge Hunt Club before Madison Square Garden and school Mrs. John J. Farrell's hunters. They would go "in-hand" and bend in the corners. Billy would regulate their strides. Now, of course, everybody rides that way, but in those days nobody did.

He would take me to Mrs. Farrell's farm, and we'd school 3-year-olds in the snow, sleet and freezing rain. He'd insist that I grab mane on young horses, not the mouth.

Billy was the person most responsible for encouraging me to try out for the U.S. Equestrian Team. During the summer of 1957, he set it up for me to ride with de Nemethy and the squad at some horse shows in this country. He was always helpful and gave me tips on how to become a better horseman, a better rider, and most of all, a better person.

He would bring me along on the lecture circuit to give after-dinner speeches on behalf of the USET. Believe it or not, I used to be tongue-tied and had terrible stage fright. Billy helped me get over that.

Fortunately for me, I rode on the USET with Billy as captain for three years. He then gave me his horse Night Owl to show, and I won the Grand Prix of Aachen (Germany) with him. There was no end to what Bill Steinkraus would do for his fellow riders, the team and the sport. He really didn't need to be anything more than an example. That was a priceless enough gift.

Nobody in our lifetime will ever equal Bill Steinkraus as an all-around horseman—hunters, jumpers, dressage, Saddlebreds, race horses, foxhunting, driving, judging and administrating. He's done it all, including writing "the" book. You would do yourself a favor if you read his latest book, *Reflections on Riding and Jumping*.

What's more, he can go to any country in the world, meet anybody from the Royal Family on down, and command instant respect. No homage due this man is enough.

Every one of us should never forget that, individually and collectively, we would not be here in the same way today if it weren't for William C. Steinkraus.

9

How Do Today's Equitation Finals Compare To The Past?

January 9, 1993

The decades come and go, and, yet, like everything in life, nothing really changes that much. Things, generally, stay pretty much the same.

Before 1950, in the supposed Dark Ages of modern riding, there were some great equitation winners, great stars of any era. Take Bill Steinkraus and Frank Chapot—they not only rode hunters and jumpers the best, but they also looked good doing it. They also went on to be Olympic champions, and they helped train others to follow in their footsteps.

The '50s were a great turning point. People were starting to take more lessons and become educated. Good form was expected. If you wanted to win, you had to be more than just a rider with a good "hunting seat" on a horse and a light pair of hands. Your heels had to be down, your eyes up, and you leaned forward. The Italian forward seat, although 50 years old, was really in vogue.

Victor Hugo-Vidal, Ronnie Mutch and I all won equitation finals in the early '50s and went on and spread the word and trained many winners ourselves. Michael Plumb and Michael Page won a little later and have more than left their stamps on the eventing world.

By the time the '60s rolled around, people were getting quite sophisticated. Bert de Nemethy's influence was already being felt in the equitation world, in addition to the teachings of Gordon Wright, Vladimir Littauer, Jimmy Williams, Chuck Grant, Wayne Carroll and many, many others.

"The average modern equitation riders are prepared to do what they do very well. But they aren't prepared to do more."

Under their influence, real flat work was being appreciated and classic gymnastic schooling of the horse was being done to cope with the more difficult courses presented at the Medal/Maclay finals in the 1960s. Some of the people who went on to great heights out of the decade include Mary Mairs Chapot, Bernie Traurig, Jimmy Kohn, Chrystine Jones Tauber, Conrad Homfeld and Katie Monahan Prudent. These people all had good, basic horsemanship backgrounds before they became equitation stars.

"We are taking the easy way out and are already paying the price."

The '70s probably produced the greatest number of equitation riders. James Hulick, Joy Slater Carrier, Buddy Brown, Leslie Burr Howard, Cynthia Hankins, Katharine Burdsall, Frances Steinwedell, Bert Mutch, Mark Leone and Laura Tidball Balisky all went on to do great things.

I do think, though, that the potential for developing all-around professional horsemen was on the wane by then.

Some of the winners of the '80s have already proven they aren't limited to the equitation ranks: Joan Scharffenberger, to name one. Ray Texel has been precocious for his age, along with Peter Wylde.

But the '80s winners, although great equitation performers, for the most part don't remind me of the riders of the past decades, good young horsemen and horsewomen who had such a broad background that they were bound to go on. These earlier riders, just in passing, won the finals. It wasn't a final accomplishment.

The '90s have gotten off to an optimistic start with Nicole Shahinian. She is a talent of any generation, now or before, male or female. Time will tell what this gifted young lady does with her talent. Another promising rider is McLain Ward, who won the USET East Coast Medal Finals in 1990.

The average modern equitation riders are prepared to do what they do very well. But they aren't prepared to do more. They have precious little in their background to prepare them to go on as Olympic team members, professionals, teachers or trainers. The young people of today are shallower, more fragile horsemen than those before.

Of course, this is our fault. We are their teachers and mentors. It is our job to teach them about "the horse" and to live with the horse again. We don't live with our horses.

And so, while it appears everything is harder, better and more sophisticated in today's equitation finals, it is not better from the view of the long-term goals. The tail is wagging the dog.

The Medal/Maclay finals are no longer an important stepping stone toward a glorious future. They're now a very big end in themselves. Winning the finals today simply means one little aspect of horsemanship has been tested—riding a trappy, rather low set of temporary fences. What used to mean one wonderful, victorious moment during the winner's long lifetime of involvement with horses is now often the end of his or her riding career.

This is sad and not how it should be. Perhaps the cycle will swing back a bit, and we'll see the simpler values of old. If we are to develop future generations of great horsemen and horsewomen, it must be. We are taking the easy way out and are already paying the price.

10

The World Cup Courses Were Back To The Future

May 5, 1995

Olaf Peterson's excellent courses for the FEI World Cup Final showed that, in a sense, we have come full circle back to the 1950s and the "rub" era, in which touches counted. The only thing we old-timers miss are the judges in the middle of the ring signaling a front or hind rub.

In those days, we didn't have a time allowed or big spreads, combinations and technical lines. But these fences are similar in that they are straight up and down and airy.

Peterson adds another dimension to this trappy airiness by placing unusual bases under the rails and elaborate, colorful wings alongside the fences. This tends to distract the horses from the top rails, so they come tumbling down. Peterson has an almost futuristic approach to course building.

The quality and quantity of European horseflesh is most impressive over these courses. This is due to the injection of Thoroughbred blood, which we have in abundance but don't seem to know how to use. The old-fashioned, powerful but heavy cart horse simply doesn't have the class to go the distance. The future of show jumping belongs to the light, intelligent, "catty" animal.

We have better horses than we realize, but they're jumped too much, both in and out of the competition ring. I strongly believe that horses have only so many jumps in them, and that's that!

The first leg of the World Cup Final is supposed to be a Table A (jump-off type course) under Table C rules (faults converted into time). Lately the course designers have been building a partly Table C course—that's OK, but it's not sticking strictly to the rules. Nonetheless, this first course was an excellent one, big enough with some good striding and turning options.

The Europeans aren't afraid to take a chance, and they simply outrode us North Americans. Unfortunately, our show managers, apparently reluctant toward any kind of change, rarely offer our grand prix horses and riders a big speed class the first time in the ring. We simply need practice doing this sort of thing.

The second leg is a one jump-off class. The course was hard and walked hard, but eight were clear. Most of the lines rode short to a wide oxer or short to a high vertical. Peterson uses lots of gymnastic-style lines and combinations, which is historically German. They're built to cater to the control of their riders and the scope of their horses.

Franke Sloothaak gave everyone a riding lesson aboard his wall-eyed, chestnut mare Weihaiwej. He galloped fast and never picked up the reins. It was a spectacular win, and he looked to me that night as if he'd win the whole thing.

The European standard of riding, training and horse management has a lot to do with the fact they've emulated our base. Most of these countries have adopted some form of an equitation or hunter division, and they have many top instructors and trainers now who give clinics and are dedicated to doing it right.

The one big difference is that the Europeans use this base only as preparation for international competition. It's rarely an end in itself. Things are kept more in perspective, the way we used to do it.

"In a sense, we have come full circle back to the 1950s and the 'rub' era."

The World Cup's third leg is a two-round competition with lighter and wider fences. The crux of the course for the first round came early on. It was a real gymnastic: oxer to oxer, 25 feet apart; then 49 feet to an airy vertical, then 34 1/2 feet to another vertical.

In the second round this line became oxer, 60 feet to a vertical, 25 feet to a square oxer, 35 feet to another vertical. Both of these lines required tremendous scope, rideability and careful jumping. These were both excellent courses.

I never remember a World Cup Final fluctuating as much as this one. First it looked like Eddie Macken, then Michael Whitaker and Franke Sloothaak, and finally Nick Skelton. Nick held his cool and used his mare the best. He didn't try to be a hero any one day. He deserved the win.

"We have better horses than we realize, but they're jumped too much."

Nick is certainly one of the best horsemen of the century. He's often placed high in championships but never won one. Nick is always training his horses to play the game. I love the way he gallops, turns and drops his horses to a short distance. He gets all his horses very clever and obedient and stays off their backs and their mouths much of the time.

We Americans had a respectable show. Lisa Jacquin, Leslie [Howard] and Beezie [Madden] ended up in the bottom half of the top 20, which is an accomplishment. McLain Ward ended up 10th and rode nothing short of brilliantly for a 19-year-old. McLain appears to have taken the best of both worlds, American and European, and combined them. He understands the overall horsemanship that is involved and manages his horse Orchestre's career beautifully. He could easily represent us in next year's Olympics.

Chris Kappler, with Zanzibar, was our highest-placed finisher, in sixth place. Chris imported this Dutch gelding as a young horse, sold him, and now is back on the horse. Chris has always been a winner who rides with class and style. He reminds me of Conrad Homfeld, which is what Marcia Williams and I thought judging him in the AHSA Medal Final some years ago.

We have the riders. Now let's give them the international experience and horses they so deserve. Medals next year in Atlanta are not out of the question.

11

Horsemanship Here And Abroad

July 7, 1995

Traveling to other countries gives me a chance to reflect and compare. It gives me the opportunity to see what we do better and what others do better.

In many ways we have the greatest overall standard of basic horsemanship in the world. Our general horse care and basic stable management is second to none. Our veterinarians, blacksmiths and equine dentists, on average, cannot be beaten. And our standard of riding, teaching and training—especially at the elementary and intermediate levels as far as jumping is concerned—is far better than any other country I've visited.

So, where can we improve?

All professionals and teachers in the United States are guilty of producing a generation of "hands-off" horsemanship. We have become good at being specialists, and so good at delegating tasks to other specialists that we only know how to do one or two things well. We are all either owners, riders, trainers, grooms, veterinarians, horse dealers, van drivers, etc. And not many of us—especially the younger generation—are good at most or all of these jobs.

The horsemen of old were perhaps not the instructors of today. Yet they knew more about the horse himself. They were "hands-on" horsemen. First of all, by their mentors, they were taught how to select a horse, to judge his conformation and way of going, as well as his jumping ability.

They developed an "eye" for a horse. They understood a horse's structural beauties as well as his structural weaknesses, both affecting the horse's ability to stand the test of time. Now, often, people buy horses by the jump alone, which is a big mistake. They buy a horse that can jump one big fence.

The selection, care and management of a horse's career are what it's all about. Anybody can ride and jump; that's not the real challenge. Once someone is lucky enough to find a good horse, then it's up to that person to care for the horse and not ruin him. Many good horses are lost to bad care and management.

Modern drugs are the best and the worst. They're the best because they do so much for the horse. And they're the worst because they're often substituted for good care and good judgment. Drugs can cover up so many things.

Where are the "leg men" of years ago? They've all but died off. With the FEI's stricter medication rules, riders showing in Europe must go back to tending their horses the old-fashioned way. They must become aware of soundness and be able to keep their horses going without relying too much on modern drugs.

The horse's management and career is influenced by many things: general and basic care, feeding, weight, temperament, shoeing, fitness and condition, flatwork, galloping work, amount of jumping, when and where to show.

Due to the modern drugs we rely on and to greed, we tend to ask too much. We practice too much (for the good of the rider, perhaps, but not the horse), and we show too much.

Again, if a person is lucky enough to stumble upon a good horse and smart enough to buy him, he won't be a good horse for long. He'll deteriorate. In fact, there are great riders in our country, and in every country, who always "run through" their horses. That's always been the way, and it's a shame.

Perhaps our biggest problem in competing with the rest of the world—as far as show jumping is concerned—is that we have a sketchy breeding program. If jumpers could be scientifically bred, like we do our race horses, we'd be on top again. We've got the riders, but not always the horses. The Europeans get the pick of the litter. Americans go to Europe and buy what they don't want for a very inflated price.

It costs too much to make a horse at home. Professionals must take green horses on the road with the rest of the barn, often to the big horse shows, and it's simply too expensive, and with so little hope of any prize money.

The Europeans have a young-horse network for producing green horses that costs them little money. Once a horse has come up through the ranks and has made it, then he goes into the string of an international rider. This a more efficient and economical way. We've got to have a cheaper way to develop horses.

As long as the equitation division is considered by most riders and trainers to be an end to itself, it will be counter-productive and defeat its purpose. The real point of this division is to help produce better young horsemen and horsewomen.

There's too much mannered, artificial, weak and stiff riding in this division—riding that will not help young riders cope in the real world later on. Youngsters around the world are often short on polish, yet strong on practicality. We, in the United States, often see it the other way around.

Hickstead, England, reminds me of how we've lost and forgotten outdoor equitation. From the pony division and up, they're jumping natural fences in the wide, open spaces. Stride counting has little value when attacking banks, ditches and hedges.

"Many good horses are lost to bad care and management."

Most of the world is following our example and becoming ring-bound. This, in turn, causes, too much emphasis on collection, dressage and sitting in the middle. Our primary problem today is that we never really get out of the ring. We are rarely given a chance to get off our horses' backs, gallop over uneven terrain, and jump a variety of fences.

Constant ring work, and jumping miniature triple bars in the hunter divisions, stifles instinct, heart and feel. There is too much thinking and analyzing in our show ring today, not just plain doing. We need to produce hunter horsemen who still retain a good degree of style and polish.

"There is too much thinking and analyzing in our show ring today, not just plain doing."

To alter direction and improve horsemanship at home, I'd like to see: 1) More "hands-on" activity with the horse; 2) A study of the selection, care and handling of the horse by professionals and amateurs alike; 3) Less reliance on horse drugs and more reliance on common sense (as far as too much drilling and jumping);

4) Our own supply of sport horses; 5) Pressure placed on show management to allow us to develop young horses economically; 6) The equitation division kept in perspective—as a means, not an end; 7) The hunters and equitation riders out of the ring whenever possible.

In some respects, we've positioned ourselves into a corner regarding these points. It's up to the intelligent, young, imaginative leaders of the sport to implement some progressive departures.

One thing that always impresses me when traveling abroad is that we've got more, better grand prix riders than any other country. This should make us proud, and we should keep on building.

12

It's Time For America To Lead The Way Again In Course Design

September 8, 1995

I'm concerned with the direction and some of the trends in course building today, at home and, especially, in Europe.

Course designers have a tremendous responsibility. They guide us to how we ride, teach and train, both in the hunter/ equitation ring and in the jumper ring. The course the designer sets ultimately teaches riders how to ride and horses how to go. We as teachers and trainers are obligated at home to prepare horses and riders for what they're to encounter at the show, not less and usually not much more.

Course designers set the direction for our whole sport. Bert de Nemethy did this in 1984 in the Los Angeles Olympics, and Olaf Peterson did it again in the 1988 Seoul Olympics. We're counting on Linda Allen to do it once more in Atlanta. She must alter some of the trends and extremes that have come into fashion over the last few years.

The principles of course design are as old as time. Fence construction, speeding up, slowing down and turning all have their roots in natural cross-country riding and hunting. We must never forget where our sport came from. A ring, be it large or small, is simply a convenient, contained area in which to hold a competition between horses and riders supposedly able to go from point A to point B across open country.

Once we stray too far from this basic principle, the sport becomes contrived and artificial.

Bert de Nemethy was the very best during the height of his career at maintaining this natural beauty in all his work. And he did it in his riding, training and teaching, as well as in his course design. It was simply his whole persona, to be as natural as possible with horses and riders. That was the real secret to his success in *everything* he did.

Imagination, combined with this natural approach to horsemanship, is the cornerstone to successful course design. Course designers' imaginations compel them to produce *variety*, the *sine qua non* of all courses.

Why is variety so important? Because it produces boldness and forward riding, the first and most important step in all riding. That the horse and rider go forward, no matter what, has always been sacred to all horsemen.

Without the natural variety, very little boldness is asked of horse or rider. And, consequently, little forward riding is developed. I emphasize the world natural. Cute, artificial, gimmicky fences need not be a part of any course, for hunters or jumpers. Occasionally, a trick fence is acceptable in an equitation class and always has been.

The fences that develop heart in the horse and rider are brush, walls, gates, coops, roll tops, panels, ditches, banks and water—all things one might encounter going from point A to point B across country.

Jumping straight up and down or jumping spread fences (composed of more than one element) is another important principles of jumping we should all understand. The real test of a jumping horse in England is his ability to get back on his hocks, slam his shoulders, jerk his knees, and jump a vertical fence clear.

This test is not quite the same when given ground lines, especially an excessive amount of ground lines, like we see in our hunter courses. Compared to European courses today, our jumpers are given too many ground lines too. Any good hunter or jumper course must ask the question of some really straight fences. But we don't like really straight fences because they expose a weakness and are harder to do.

The Germans were always known for their ability to jump width, probably because of their big, strong horses. Then we became good at jumping width. Now we don't ask our grand prix horses to jump wide enough. Jumping a real spread is a test that's apt to compromise the horse's rideability, the rider's control, and the ability to jump upcoming verticals.

Really square oxers are, probably, the hardest spread fence to jump (and we don't get enough of those either!), but all the other fences in the spread family must not be neglected.

Historically, hunter and jumper courses around the world were built around natural fences. I remember well the outside course around Devon (Pa.) with its solid and big log-and-ditch fence and its table bank. Dublin (Ireland) was known for its Irish banks. Aachen (Germany) for its "tiger trap" and double liverpools, and Lucerne (Switzerland) for its many and varied banks, ditches and hedges. Frank Chapot and I designed the natural fences used at Lake Placid (N.Y.) and in the old ring in Palm Beach (Fla.). Rotterdam (the Netherlands) had a wonderful, multi-level bank combined with spooky ditches.

Each of these shows has all but eliminated their natural fences. It's a crime and, to me, violates one of the most important principles of why we jump horses in the first place—to go from point A to point B across country.

Natural fences are too hard for people to deal with today. Show managers don't like them because they require maintenance, and that means money. Course builders don't like them because they "get in the way" of their precious lines with related distances. Trainers and riders don't like them because they take special training at home and energetic riding in the ring. These are all lame excuses.

Combinations are a principle of modern course building that has presented much discussion and controversy this summer in Europe. The English and the French like to build combinations with only straightforward, classic distances. The Germans and the Dutch are now building combinations with very short distances to very wide oxers. Common sense says that any extreme distance with a combination is a bit risky and asks for a fall. Usually a combination is enough of a problem without adding tricky distances. I like to see a variety of fences in combinations—walls, gates and liverpools. This gives variety in combinations and requires a clever, bold horse.

All courses, in principle, should have massive, solid, imposing fences (testing boldness), as well as airy and light fences (testing cleverness and respect). Without a balance between these two kinds of jumps, there is no true all-around test of a horse. I want to see the all-around ability of both horse and rider, not one or maybe two dimensions.

Our hunter fences rarely, if ever, are airy, straight-up-and-down, without ground lines anymore. There is nothing today like the gate fences used years ago at the old Madison Square Garden (N.Y.) in what was known as course "K." Those kinds of jumps really tested a hunter's front end.

"Historically, hunter and jumper courses around the world were built around natural fences."

Europe has gone to the other extreme. Everything today, even at Aachen, is airy and light.

Course builders the world over today, no matter what discipline, understand the principle of testing a horse's rideability. The ability of the horse to lengthen, shorten and turn left and right is at the top of the agenda, and it should be. Again, unless a course builder has a good feel for riding a course, these tracks can become artificial and abrupt, not allowing for a smooth performance by the horse and rider. A horseman's track is always the most enjoyable to ride.

"Without balance, there is no true all-around test of a horse."

What should a good hunter course be? First, the fence material must be as natural yet attractive as possible. The fence must, according to the rules, simulate those found in the hunting field. For the most part, I find our fence material in the United States first class.

What I do not agree with is the catering to the mediocre, limited horse or rider by the overuse of ground lines.

71

Anything testing, demanding or uncomfortable for the horse, rider, judge, course builder or show manager is quickly eliminated. In America today, comfort and ease are what is demanded and expected. Hunter riders—pony riders, juniors, amateurs or professionals—never have the opportunity to learn to jump really straight-up-and-down fences. Most every obstacle is a low, triple bar-like fence. Everybody knows a triple bar is an easy fence to jump and covers up a multitude of sins. That's one of the reasons there's so much flat jumping and "stepping" in our show rings. Again, variety is being lost and forgotten.

Except for the fact that our jumper courses are not high and wide enough, the imagination of our course designers is better than those in Europe. I was a bit disappointed this summer in the sameness of the European jump material, coupled with the fact that they've discarded so many of their natural fences.

Europe is encouraging—I would really say demanding— backward riding, or what we used to call "hand-riding," something we have so long tried to get away from. Almost every line is extremely tight, requiring the rider to pull up and add a stride or two, usually throughout the entire course. Control and collection, it appears, is about all they're interested in. And what's suffering is the horse's bascule. Again, variety is being lost in the interest of expediency.

I have great confidence in Linda Allen's designs for the Olympic Games next summer in Atlanta. Linda is a top horsewoman and rode well at a high level. She has a great feel for both the horse and the rider. She was brought up in the old school of horsemanship and, I know, values many of the old principles of riding, training and course building. Yet she has kept up to date and is always on the road, both here and abroad.

Linda is a woman who keeps on learning about her craft. I

really believe she'll test all of the horses' and riders' abilities, not just some. She's not a horsewoman of extremes when it comes to repeatedly pulling horses up and jumping very wide fences off backward strides. And I know her work well enough to know she'll appreciate and use natural fences whenever and wherever possible.

Let's again be leaders in the world of course design. Nobody ever did it better than our own Bert de Nemethy. We can do it again.

13

Our Shows Should Be Much, Much More

January 5, 1996

I was so frustrated when I returned from Monterrey, Mexico, and Calgary, Alberta, this fall that I felt I had to do something. When I compared these two international shows to our biggest shows, ours came up far short.

So I called Eric Straus, a friend who is the assistant executive director of the American Horse Shows Association, and vented my plight. He suggested I talk to the show managers, who were meeting soon at the National Horse Show. This I did, not to win any popularity contest but to discuss some of what I see as the problems of horse shows in America. Most of these managers are old friends and appeared to listen carefully and be most receptive.

We all know that the hunter/jumper in this country is in trouble. I've been on the A-rated circuit as a rider, owner and trainer for almost 50 years, and I know we have some big problems that at least need to be addressed.

There is a decline from every aspect. Most horse shows have lost their individuality, appeal, and just plain class. The open jumper division and the grand prix courses are often so watered down to accommodate the weaker riders and horses that they're unrecognizable. The style in the equitation division is not what we were taught. That's certainly gone down. And, to be perfectly frank, so has our Olympic team.

The reason is because we always cater to the lowest common denominator. When you do that, you become mediocre. And mediocre is what we've become, compared to many other countries, when it comes to horse showing.

In the United States we do a good job showing, but not a great job. There is such a big difference. Yes, we've got everything in place to produce the best. When you are the richest country on earth, have a tradition of great horsemen and horsemanship, have some potentially fabulous facilities, great teachers, trainers, riders, owners, veterinarians, blacksmiths and course designers, what more could you want?

But we have too many shows, especially bad shows. I don't know the pros and cons of the AHSA's "mileage" rule. I'm an exhibitor and owner, not a show manager. I do know that most show managers love the mileage rule, however. It protects them. Most exhibitors would do away with the mileage rule, forcing the shows to freely compete, which would automatically produce quality. Only the best ones would survive.

In Europe this free-enterprise system puts the quality of every show constantly on the line. Each weekend has so many good shows that only the very best stand a chance.

Some of the criteria are: facility, hospitality, footing, course builder, types of classes, prize money, stabling, and location. If any are lacking, the top riders simply don't go.

Several years ago I spoke on this subject at an AHSA convention forum. I said of the bad horse shows, "Death is a wonderful thing!" I was tarred and feathered and railroaded out of the forum. Consequently I haven't been to a convention since. I have more constructive things to do.

Walter J. (Jimmy) Lee is a great old friend of mine. He always stressed the word "show" in horse show. Where has the "show" gone in our horse shows? Even hunter classes used to be glamorous. All that is gone. It's gotten monotonous and dreary. American shows, save for a couple of events like the American Invitational, are boring. There is little or no thrill in our shows. They're useful for us exhibitors, but that's where it stops. We must put theater back into our horse shows.

Today's horse shows aren't building our sport. Because we are paying for our own game, costs are becoming increasingly prohibitive. Today's hunter/jumper game is really only for the very rich or the rare, very talented minor pro.

I'm fairly successful in this business and can barely afford to carry a horse or two down the road anymore. Years ago I had initially owned, trained and shown many of my clients' top horses in the hunter and jumper division. After I'd make them at my own expense, I sold them on. All of us professionals will tell you the same thing: We cannot afford to show our own horses anymore. No wonder so few great horses are being made. That's why we're frustrated.

What's wrong in America? Why can Canada, Mexico and Europe put on better shows than we can? Why are their shows so high class and "smartly" produced? Why can they get sponsorship and tens of thousands of spectators to pay the bills for us to perform? Why don't I see our horse show managers at these foreign shows, especially on our own doorstep, learning and studying? Monterrey and Calgary and Aachen (Germany) are learning experiences for me, and I'm not a show manager.

Sallie Wheeler, president of the National Horse Show, just sent manager David Distler to Maastricht (the Netherlands) and Olympia (England) to observe and learn. That is an intelligent approach. We all learn from people who do it better and know more. That's what more show managers should be doing.

"I'm tired of the excuses people make and the bills I have to pay."

The show organizers abroad are important and powerful people because they're responsible for a big event. The most successful shows are promoted to and supported by the hometown, its public and its business community. We see that recipe work especially well at Devon (Pa.) and the Hampton Classic (N.Y.). This approach must be explored more closely. The pride of each town is what makes every show in Europe so special and so successful.

The three-foot divisions are both good and bad. Yes, they are a wonderful thing for people and horses who shouldn't jump higher, and they help pay the bills. But they have no place at major or championship events, where time and space are limited and the management hopes to draw spectators.

"We always cater to the lowest common denominator."

I'm sorry to say it, but those low divisions have helped lower our standards. People will always opt to go lower. It's easier and maybe safer. But perhaps they could go higher and surprise themselves. But, again, we're catering to the lowest common denominator.

Our established managers and the young horse show managers coming into the business must develop a different mentality. A horse show must be looked at as a community effort, putting on a spectator/sponsor-friendly event that also happens to serve the exhibitors. It must be two shows in one. Most of our shows cater 90 percent to us exhibitors and a measly 10 percent to the outside world. A much, much bigger percentage of thought, imagination and effort must go into the "show" part of it to attract the uninvolved.

I'm tired of the excuses people make, the bills I have to pay, and the decline in my sport and passion—horse showing. Let's see the show managers, their committees and support groups at least try to fix it and put the word "show" back into the game.

There is a lot more to horse showing than the average fare we're exposed to week after week. If you don't believe me, just look around. If we continue with this apathetic inertia, we will stay a second-rate horse community and get back what we deserve—not much.

14

We Have The Riders, Now We Need To Develop The Horses

February 7, 1997

To me, the results of 1996 and our future in horse showing depend on six factors: horse shows, horses, Olympic trials, the Olympics themselves, the fall indoor shows and equitation.

HORSE SHOWS: Yes, I believe we have a method to prepare horses and riders to compete over fences that's as good or even better than anywhere in the world. No country can start a rider so correctly (in short stirrup or maiden equitation) and take them up to classes like the American Invitational or the American Gold Cup.

Where else can a horse start out so gently in the pre-green hunter division or schooling divisions and end up on our Olympic team, after all the various steps in between? Probably nowhere.

There is no place else on earth I'd rather make a horse or rider. We're so organized in the stepping stones and building blocks. Other countries envy our structure.

And our average show is good to many other countries. Again the structure of organization, stabling, footing, veterinary services, fence material, and courses in America are predictable and more than satisfactory.

That's the good news. The bad news is the general apathy at generic horse shows. When the same horse show travels from week to week and place to place, an apathetic attitude must set in. It is the sameness and the boredom, even if what's offered is quite good.

Usually, the best horse shows are fresh horse shows. A new town, a new venue, a new ring and set of fences, and some different faces, both inside and outside of the ring.

The best horse shows are always a community effort. The community is behind the show and often runs the show. There is a certain pride in this kind of show.

The worst news of all nowadays is the expense involved in showing horses, both for amateurs and professionals. People like me can no longer "help out" young riders, carrying them and their horses down the road. It is simply far too costly.

As a young professional, I always owned or took on horses for the likes of Conrad Homfeld, Katie Monahan Prudent, Leslie Burr Howard and Melanie Smith Taylor to ride. It helped me make the horses, and it helped them learn to ride. Those days are long gone. There is something

"There is no place on earth I'd rather make a horse or rider."

"The best horse shows are always a community effort."

very wrong when I don't feel I can afford to carry a young horse to Florida to help out a young rider who can't quite afford it. It's now more than ever a sport for the very rich.

Yes, the managers, all good friends of mine, do a great job for us. But they're caught up on a treadmill, going faster and faster on the same path.

In all other countries the man off the street, the paying public, the sponsors and TV are considered first and foremost, even ahead of the stars like Ludger Beerbaum, Franke Sloothaak, and John Whitaker. In our country it appears the public is thought of last, almost as an afterthought.

Yes, the exhibitors are terribly important. The owners, amateurs, professionals and juniors make the show. But unless we figure how to do it a little differently, we will continue to pay for it all ourselves. Our current crop of managers is so "in the groove" in the way they do things, I don't know if they could change even if they wanted to.

I am a teacher. And to be a teacher I've always had to be a learner. It's very perplexing to me never to see our horse show managers learning in Calgary (Alta.), Monterrey (Mexico), Aachen (Germany), Hickstead (England), Dublin (Ireland) or many other European shows. Our sport is constantly changing. And to keep up one must keep on looking, listening and learning.

One thing is for sure: If our sport is to grow and thrive, and maybe even survive, we must be more imaginative in showing off show jumping to the public.

The National Horse Show's return to New York's Madison Square Garden was (and hopefully will continue to be) a shot in the arm for our game. Thanks to Sallie Wheeler, Charles Dolan and Alan Balch, we have a chance at a showcase indoor horse show. Yes, it does have to get tightened up; yes, we do need more spectacular exhibitions (although Cigar will be hard to follow up); yes, they do need to aim for a $1 million jumper division to attract the biggest names in the world. But you cannot tell me New York City can't afford to make this one of the richest shows in the world.

The world is a small place today. Everybody goes to Calgary. Everybody goes to Monterrey. Of course, everybody should come here. Sometimes, with our limited thinking and limited pocketbooks, we act like second-class citizens. Come on, horse show managers, think big and think theater. There is a way to get people other than us to help pay the bills. Others do it every week. We just have to learn how and go to work.

HORSES: We have the best system in the world to teach large numbers of people how to ride. We could have fielded four Olympic teams that might have done well. We take better care of our horses on average. Our veterinarians and blacksmiths are second to none.

What we cannot do is supply the athlete, the one jumping the fence, the horse, as far as international competition is concerned. Our No. 1 problem is the horseflesh. We have the riders, and we can continue to make them. But we must do whatever it takes to establish an internal supply of horses for those riders. This, I know, is a very difficult task. We are way behind other countries in our breeding program. Katie and Henri Prudent were just judging young horses in Brazil. They were astounded at the quality and quantity of the animals they saw. Brazil was third in show jumping in Atlanta and fourth in the 1994 World Championships. They too will be beating us soon—because of their sporthorse breeding programs.

You know who my newest heroes and friends are? Anybody trying to breed hunters and jumpers. These are the people who are going to enable us to win. Let's top the Thoroughbred market again. We must concentrate hard now on *the horse*. The riders are doing OK.

OLYMPIC TRIALS: As long as there are selection trials for the Olympics or other international championships, people will disagree on how to select the team. Now that the subjective/ objective subject is behind us, the disagreement will continue over the format of the trials and the time frame. This year, while we got a good result at the Olympics, the complaint was that the trials were too long and drawn out and that horses came fresh off the farm every time.

My feeling is that one-round trials really serve no purpose. They have nothing to do with the actual format of an Olympic Games or a World Championships. A trial of two or three rounds while the horses are stabled together in a secure location is far more realistic.

I do feel strongly, though, that if we're going to use the objective system, there must be three trials of equal difficulty. If there are too few rounds or one or two courses are too soft, the wrong results are likely to happen. This year, right down to the 16th horse, I thought we got a perfect order of finish.

THE OLYMPICS: Atlanta proved that we're not leaving all the others in the dust. Atlanta, Monterrey and the developing riders tour gave us all confidence that we're very competitive at the top level, but we're not really beating them yet. As Anne Kursinski put it so well: "I want to beat you guys [the Germans]!" And so do I.

Our success in Atlanta should spur us on. It should make our grand prix riders look for owners and for horses. That, of course, is the first step. Then they must train and bring along their horses properly. And then they must win. And I don't mean win in the backyard where it's easy, but win where it counts against the "Big Boys."

Speaking of the "Big Boys," the U.S. Equestrian Team has three show jumping tours on the agenda for 1997, two for the elite riders and one for the developing riders. All the shows planned are of major importance. Even the developing riders' tour will be a bit more difficult so as to learn more from stiffer competition. All of these riders will be selected off the USET computer list, objectively.

The object of this European assault is to prepare as many horses and riders as possible for the 1998 World Equestrian Games. These riders will also have a leg up in experience for the selection trials. There is, unfortunately, no substitute in any of our international disciplines for European experience. It is a tremendous sacrifice, I know, for all taking part in these tours, both riders and owners. But it must be done. It's the No. 1 priority.

THE FALL SHOWS: Our four fall indoor shows must maintain their standards. Harrisburg, Washington, New York and Toronto must live up to their historic past.

Harrisburg's presentation for the AHSA Medal Finals and for the AHSA Prix des States junior jumper competition was beautifully done. The ring and fences looked good this year. It's a great ring to ride in, the stabling is marvelous, and there are good places to school and ride. Harrisburg should be proud. It's a good show. But I'm always appalled at the way spectators dress at Harrisburg today. It used to be a very glamorous audience. I guess it's just the society and fashion today.

Washington is the same. I remember being with the Newberrys (Jessica Ransehausen's parents) when they started the show around 1960. It was so glamorous. Even the President came. Washington must attend to its details and remember that it's an honor and a privilege to be awarded a CSIO status by the Federation Equestrian Internationale. They must adhere strictly to FEI rules and try to make it a world-class event.

We all knew it was wrong for the National Horse Show to leave Madison Square Garden; and we know so even more now that we're back. I predict this show will be the greatest.

I haven't been to Toronto in years, but everyone tells me it's better than ever. That is because they've been able to improve their standards. They are a committee of classy people who do things right. It's a lesson for us all to learn and re-learn. It's a question of details and beauty, not necessarily money. I see Michael Matz every day at his show, St. Christopher's (Pa.), working like a dog, getting his hands dirty, making it better for horses and more attractive for the people. That's what it's all about.

EQUITATION: Hunter seat equitation seems to be back on the right track, at least it seemed that way to me after I watched the 1996 finals. Teachers, remember it's not a pseudo-dressage seat over fences. What I appreciated this year were: shorter stirrups, heels down, ankles flexed, toes out, legs in contact, riders "up" and "down" (not always sitting down), leaning forward (not backward), and soft, following arms and hands. It's called the *forward seat,* and it's the basis of the way we ride in this country. We've done pretty well riding this way for the better part of this century. If you're lucky enough just to watch Joe Fargis (1984 Olympic individual and team gold medalist) and Susie Hutchison (1996 winner of the $50,000 Budweiser Grand Prix of New York aboard America I), both are excellent examples of correct riding with the forward seat.

These are my random thoughts as 1996 comes to a close. I have repeated many of the thoughts I've expressed throughout the year, but those who know me as a teacher know that's not an accident.

15

Values—And Boys—Are Hard To Find On Our Horse Show Scene

October 10, 1997

Anne Kursinski and I were amazed and saddened not to see one boy at all among the contestants when we judged the USET West Coast Talent Search last month. I saw the same thing a year or two ago at the Pennsylvania National.

The lack of participation by boys in our sport is a true indication of how deeply rooted our problems are in the sport. Many of the problems we see today are moral, not technical.

What are our values today in the hunter/jumper world? Let's face it, money is the root of all evil. We've attached too much importance to money. Money has nothing at all to do with equestrian sports, except to pay the bills. Unfortunately, keeping horses is and always will be an expensive hobby.

Money and greed are the worst problems that have crept in to what I used to think of as my sport. I'm afraid unless our society has a big shock, that money will be the eventual ruination of this sport as we once knew it.

What kind of sport is horse showing today? A large percentage of the riders in America are not really fit athletes. In most sports, one must be very fit. I see far too many riders soft, physically and/or mentally. Many are overweight, overfed, spoon-fed, pampered, coddled, babied and nursed. Is that the kind of atmosphere in which parents want to indulge their sons? No. Parents do not want their sons growing up in a "sissy" sport.

I would expect a father to want his son to learn *real* values: self-discipline, a take-it-on-the-chin and pick-yourself-up work ethic, sportsmanship, get tough, bravery, etc. Most of these values are hard to find today on the American horse show scene.

Yes, I have the courage to be very, very honest and critical about a situation I helped create. I've wondered if I want to perpetuate this roll downhill to nowhere. What are we as horseman and women creating and perpetuating? What values are we promoting? Do we want to keep doing this the same way? I feel much in our day-to-day horse world is most unhealthy.

I consider the "hate mail" I receive from overweight riders and readers a bad joke, as I see the fat bulging through their tailored green or blue jackets. There are very, very few "soft," overweight show jumping riders in Europe. They are lean and mean and ready for sport.

Victor Hugo-Vidal, Ronnie Mutch, and I were in the gender minority in the early 1950s, but it wasn't such a minority. Boys made up an average of 25 to 30 percent of the pony, junior hunters and equitation classes back then. Nowadays, it may be about 5 percent, and that's very sad.

The boys on ponies in those days came out of the hunting field, and that was a good, rough-and-tumble sport. They fell off, got tired, wet, and cold.

Richard Zimmerman, Sydney Gadd, Billy Boyce and Roddy

Wanamaker (to name a few) came up from Maryland and Pennsylvania to show at Madison Square Garden. They galloped and jumped. It was fast and exciting. Boys liked ponies back then. There was a degree of risk. One didn't have to be *too perfect*. Do you know how crippling it is to have to be too perfect?

Michael Plumb also came out of the hunting field to show his junior hunters and ride in equitation classes. Winning the ASPCA Maclay Finals was just a small part of his year with his horses. Michael was used to a tough way of life riding cross-country and foxhunting with his father.

Yes, there were professional women riders back in the early 1950s. But most women in those days rode as amateurs. Peggy Augustus was perhaps the most noteworthy because she could regularly beat the professional men in the hunter division. The great bulk of professionals, as in Europe today, were men. And very often their apprentices and assistants were men. Thus, the continuation of generations of horsemen. We are in danger of losing this all-important balance in the hunter/jumper world in North America.

It was harder then both physically and mentally for the girls. The hunters galloped at 16 to 18 mph over solid, 4'6" fences. Most horses certainly weren't schooled as they are today—they often had dead mouths and half ran off. It was definitely a sport for the hardy and the brave.

Bert de Nemethy, freshly arrived from Europe, was not accustomed to women riding internationally at grand prix level. Women weren't even allowed to ride jumpers in the Olympic Games until 1960. It took him five, 10, 15 years to adjust to women riding on the Olympic team. Mary Mairs Chapot, Kathy Kusner, Carol Hofmann Thompson and Chrystine Jones Tauber were a few of the early ones.

Nowadays in our country the women practically dominate. McLain Ward, Todd Minikus, Richard Spooner, Peter Leone and Peter Wylde were the only guys officially representing the USET abroad this simmer. Of 15 riders, only one-third were men.

I'm the greatest fan of our lady riders. I've probably always been proudest of my female students' accomplishments. I love it when the girls beat the European "macho" men at their own game. Often it's a girl they've never seen nor heard of before. I love it when the European superstars are scratching their heads.

The whole European scene is dominated by men, except for Sweden and possibly England—the farmers, the breeders, the teachers, the trainers, the owners, and riders. This tends to naturally encourage younger boys to participate. Many, many girls ride in the junior divisions in Europe, but as they climb the ladder and the sport gets tougher, the girls fall by the wayside. At the grand prix level women make up only about 5 percent. I attribute this to the society, priorities, and a lack of teaching skills.

What's the answer? Well, now that equitation, ponies and junior hunters have become self-indulgent, artificial, ever softer, we've got to look in other directions if boys are going to survive. Very few boys want to play the game as it is today: get out of the car; present the perfectly schooled, over-longed horse; be put on; be taught lessons ad infinitum; and never really get to enjoy the thrills of what riding and dealing with horses is all about. And few boys want to be scrutinized just for perfection's sake.

What we need for the boys—and the girls—is to develop a pony jumper division like they have in most other countries. But it has never happened here and never will. Pony jumpers do not catch on because we only think of ponies as hunters. It would take a very big effort by a large group of professionals interested in the sport, rather than in their own short-term goals.

The pony jumper division would be a wonderful first step for children, especially the boys. Of course, they could and would ride the hunters and equitation of they wanted. The European countries have national and international classes for ponies, children, juniors, and young riders before hitting the senior ranks. This is a logical progression to develop true riders for the future. Many of our girls quit after they turn 18. They're often sick of the unhealthy routine, go to college, and get married. And the boys were never there. And for good reason.

North Americans should seriously consider putting this progression in place. It would help us create riders and professionals for the future. The future of the jumping sport lies in the jumper divisions. The hunter and equitation divisions have a very important place in our sport, but our jumping sport can no longer be built around and revolve around them. Evolution and destiny are putting it the other way around. The handwriting is on the wall!

The pony jumper division would be a wonderful alternative, especially for boys who no longer wish to subject themselves to the hunter and equitation divisions. It would give us a chance to develop more men as riders and as professionals.

"Money and greed are the worst problems that have crept in to what I used to think of as my sport."

"I have the courage to be very, very honest and critical about a situation I helped create."

I don't know if I'll see a real change in this imbalance in my lifetime. But to judge such a prestigious national championship as the USET Talent Search and not see one boy is a sad state of affairs. Hap Hansen won the grand prix at the same show and gave us all a riding lesson. Let's think about all that we can do to insure that we have some Hap Hansens coming along for the future.

16

Remembering The Great d'Inzeo Brothers

July 3, 1998

Since many of us are focused on going to Italy this year for the World Equestrian Games, it's a good moment in time to remember two of the "greats"—Piero and Raimondo d'Inzeo.

By the time I first got to Europe with the U.S. Equestrian Team on the 1958 summer tour, the d'Inzeo brothers were already living legends. They made up 50 percent of the formidable Italian show jumping team, who had won scores of classes all over Europe and had also won medals at several Olympic Games. The late '50s saw them heading toward the almost inevitable, the gold and silver individual medals at the 1960 Rome Olympic Games. Rome was their hometown, and they pulled off this amazing feat, Raimondo winning the gold and Piero the silver (much like Joe Fargis and Conrad Homfeld in Los Angeles in 1984). Those kinds of accomplishments are very hard to do!

Piero and Raimondo represented the Italian system of riding at that time very well. Through their father and the cavalry, they had been well indoctrinated in the Caprilli system. They rode an extreme forward seat by today's standards. Susie Hutchison, Anne Kursinski, Joe Fargis, Katie Prudent and Nona Garson are holdovers of this seat. They ride very much *with* their horses rather than *behind* their horses in the German-Dutch style so often seen today.

But the position of the d'Inzeo brothers' legs was a bit different than we see today. Caprilli advocated a strong knee and thigh grip and rider's foot almost "home" in the stirrup. This stirrup position makes it harder to flex the ankle and depress the heels. Their heels were not down as we see riders' heels down today. It was a different leg.

The modern leg position, with the "grip" put into the calf, must have been introduced by the French during the last century. The French authors recommend this position in their literature, and I much prefer it. Every other school in Europe taught a strong knee and thigh grip. We in America distribute the contact evenly between the thigh, inner knee bones, and the calf of the leg, much like the French.

However, in every other respect the d'Inzeo brothers adhered to the forward seat as we know it, with the upper body inclined well forward and a straight line from the elbow to the mouth, along with very short stirrups.

I was mesmerized when I first saw the two d'Inzeos. Up until that time, my "foreign" hero had been Gen. Humberto Mariles Cortez, a 1948 double gold medalist who captained the successful Mexican team. Mariles also galloped and followed his horses to their fences and didn't interfere too much. I always liked this approach and still do today.

But it was time to change idols. Not only were Piero and Raimondo d'Inzeo winning everything in sight in Europe, but they also rode very much according to the principles I'd been taught for so long by Gordon Wright. I could really relate to the forward seat way of riding much more than to the German style. And I've never changed my tastes and preferences when it comes to horsemanship. People need to hear and see different styles of riding today and different approaches to training.

"I was mesmerized when I first saw the two d'Inzeos."

Actually, it was quite amazing how differently these two brothers approached riding and training. And this was quite noticeable in those days. Raimondo was known as the bigger winner and Piero as the theoretician. But each won a great deal and was an extraordinarily principled horseman. What were the differences?

Raimondo appeared to adjust his style to his many different kinds of horses. Piero seemed to mold all of his mounts to his system. Raimondo, as I remember, liked any type of horse, but especially hot, Italian Thoroughbreds. Piero seemed to prefer big, particularly Irish half-breds. But they could and did ride any horse superbly.

"Piero *always* followed his horses out of the corner and allowed them to set themselves."

Raimondo was probably a more flexible trainer. He compromised with these hot horses. Piero was a more rigid disciplinarian. Horses had to go his way, and when they did they were hard to beat.

In those days Raimondo was known as a "hand rider"—he manipulated his horses to their fences. This was strictly against the Caprilli doctrine, which Piero followed to the letter. Raimondo nipped, grabbed, and set up his horses on the way to a jump. He was a master of the pulley rein. Piero *always* followed his horses out of the corner and allowed them to set themselves. He jumped many fixed obstacles to teach his horses to do this.

While I've always admired both of these men tremendously, as a rider and as a trainer I've always tried to emulate Piero. He was so rigid in his principles and beliefs, so unbendable. My character is much like that, and I guess that's why I was so attracted to this man's horsemanship. He has had a most profound influence on my own riding, teaching and training techniques.

The d'Inzeo brothers last competed internationally in 1977, but I've discussed them here because we should never forget equestrian history and the greats of our sport. It's especially important that we remember these two genius horseman who have indirectly given so much of their talent to all of us living here in the United States.

17

1998 Showed The Limitations Of The Industry We've Created

February 5, 1999

We, the devotees of the sport of riding hunters, jumpers and equitation, have created, for better or for worse, a huge industry. This evolution from sport toward business has taken place rather dramatically during the 50 years since the end of World War II.

But we must remember that we're all part of a bigger world, a world called horsemanship. Horsemanship involves the handling of any horse or pony of any size, breed, or discipline anywhere in the world.

Horsemanship was very simple when it took hold of me as a youngster in those post-war days: Taking care of ponies in one's own backyard, driving around town with a horse and buggy, riding to local shows, standing horses in cold brooks, jumping bareback, and dealing with much, much simpler medication and training techniques. Horsemanship has evolved, like most everything else, into an extremely complete, technical, specialized job.

Maybe the horses are better off. Yet most old-timers agree—something has been lost. We have lost some naturalness and spontaneity in dealing with horses. Grooming used to be a pleasurable and intimate moment of quality time with one's horse. Now there is hardly any time. We're all too busy. It must be left to grooms, who are often very good. But it's not the same.

It seems nowadays one must be very sophisticated to be able to even hack a horse, let alone teach, train or show a horse over fences. Years ago it was a rare, unusual and serious occurrence when you called the veterinarian. I often see trainers and riders now who dare not school or show their horses without their vets and blacksmiths in constant attendance.

Buck Brannaman and I just did a clinic with Rodney Jenkins, the consummate American horseman of the 20th century. Rodney knows conformation and structure of a horse, how a horse should move. He knows soundness and how to take care of legs. Nobody rode, schooled, or showed a horse better than Rodney. Nobody won more than Rodney, on a hunter or a jumper. Rodney is a horseman with immense scope and range.

With each generation since the war I see less scope and range. Yes, we have wonderful teachers, trainers and riders who are very good in their world. Too often, however, they are limited. They need to broaden their horizons. This is the big price we pay for specialization.

I very much hope that the 21st century will bring about the re-emergence of horsemanship as an art, rather than just riding. We'll be better off for it.

Horse shows today are a far cry from those sleepy, leisurely, social, elegant sporting events of the 1950s. The numbers have taken over—people, exhibitors, horses and dollars. And these numbers have increased so dramatically that time and space has diminished.

Historically, horse shows were founded on a sporting, social, amateur, competitive structure. Gradually, due to costs and a modern business mentality, horse shows around the world have taken on a business mantle. After World War II, though, American horse shows took one fork in this business-oriented road and the rest of the world took another fork. The road we took, possibly out of necessity, states that we, the players, must pay to play. This is a very shortsighted premise with endless financial and negative repercussions.

The rest of the world at least tries to put on a show for the spectators, sponsors and TV. We'll be in trouble until we change. The biggest problem that I see is that the best American potential—both young horse and young rider—cannot financially afford to develop within our system. None of us professionals can afford to make young horses like we used to. And it's much more difficult for talented young people to get a leg up today than, say, 30 years ago.

I began my teaching career with my nephew and nieces riding ponies, so I remember the division quite well. I hear stories today about the pony ring, and I'm sure they are quite true: Little princes and princesses running around being bad sports, with parents and trainers being even worse sports! It is not the kids' fault. It is the fault of the parents and the trainers if they are badly mannered.

The values must always be horsemanship, not money, blue ribbons or even talent. Brats around the pony ring only reflect on their elders.

The junior hunter division is a graduating step up from the pony division. Again, specialization has taken over. Fewer and fewer junior hunters double as equitation horses. Up until the early 1980s many of the Maclay/Medal winners were aboard their champion hunters. Now, it seems, most juniors need at least one and sometimes two or three horses for each division.

Years ago, the only time you jumped a three-foot fence in a rated show was in a novice or limit equitation class. Green horses showed over 3 feet in the spring schooling shows. Devon (Pa.) was after their first A-rated show, and they jumped 3'6".

Now the divisions that fill the most are the three-foot ones— or even lower! From the point of view of teaching and business, it's good. But the big picture is bad. Most of these horses and riders don't realize their potential. Many could easily jump 3'6", even 4 feet. But over time we've lowered our standards.

Perhaps the saddest thing that has happened to our sport over the past five decades is what has happened to the working and conformation hunter divisions. I remember only too well big, scopey, Thoroughbred horses galloping and jumping big, solid, straight-up-and-down fences, bending their knees and cracking their backs. No, performances were not as studied nor as perfect as today. However, they represented what this sport is all about—galloping across country over unfamiliar terrain, over big, solid, varied, natural obstacles.

The open hunter division has lost its luster, lost its sporting appeal. For this reason it's dying. My suggestion is to introduce big-money hunter classes on a regular basis. It costs so much today to show a horse that there must be a financial incentive for the open hunter.

By losing the hunter divisions, we've lost a lot. It's hurt our riding. Riding a big four-foot or 4'6" hunter course is a great riding experience. It's also hurt our chances to develop horses that could go on to bigger and better things. Years ago, many of our top international jumpers came out of the hunter division.

How many international jumpers of late have been first produced as hunters?

There has been an about-face in my lifetime. Years ago, the hunters took center stage and the jumpers were the scruffy stepchildren. Now the jumpers have taken over. It's given people financial, riding and political options. The hunter community has given the store away to the jumper people.

Unfortunately, our open jumper division is being watered down like our open hunter division. Often the courses aren't the size they should be. Again, money rears its ugly head. The show managers want the open and grand prix courses modified to accommodate weaker and green riders, lesser and greener horses. Again, this catering to the lowest common denominator lowers our standards. The open jumper division must hold firm like it did in the 1960s, 1970s and 1980s. We must rise to our expectations. This is one of the many reasons we are not as strong internationally as we should be.

Take a look at our international teams. Yes, we are doing OK—but just OK. Winning a silver medal in the 1996 Atlanta Olympics, winning the Samsung Nations Cup series in 1997, and cleaning up at Monterrey (Mexico) in October are not shoddy accomplishments. Yet, how can these wins compare to the de Nemethy years (1955-1980)? Or the 1980s, when we made a clean sweep of the medals in the 1984 Los Angeles Olympics, won the 1986 World Championships in Aachen (Germany), and, between us and the Canadians, won every FEI World Cup Finals during the 1980s?

The decade of the 1990s has shown a marked decline in American show jumping. The rest of the world cannot believe this happened.

First to blame for our international decline is our standards

101

and self-discipline in general. This includes the standard of teaching for all-around horsemanship here in America. On this front, the Europeans are ahead of us every day. The European shows do not cater to the middle or lowest common denominator. Your horsemanship must meet their standards.

Second to blame is the unacceptable cost of showing horses in America. Only the very rich can afford to produce young horses today. And even they can't, so the professional has no hope. This has driven most of our horse dealers out of business and forced all of us to spend our money in Europe. This domino affect is a crying shame. It is very hard to get the very best horses out of Europe to mount our wonderful American riders. The Europeans want these horses for themselves to beat us. We must be allowed by horse show managers to be able to bring young horses along.

Third to blame is the rigid procedures used to put teams together. We cannot put teams together without some flexibility—if we want to win again on a predictable and consistent basis. Our results of the last decade reflect rigidity, rather than our potential to win. We should be winning more, much more. But until this generation of active athletes figures it out, we will all be continually disappointed. It's too bad because the rest of the world alternates between laughing at us and crying for us.

102

Having witnessed the last 50 years at close range, I see a general malaise and decline. We are not very sick, but we are sick. I'm afraid the good has been outweighed just a little bit by the bad. We are the greatest and richest casualty in the world. We are steeped in a tradition of excellent horsemanship. We must get back to our old work ethic, "think big," get rid of politics, raise our standards to where they should be, and figure it out. The world is giving us a wake-up call by doing it all better than we do, and we'd better get off our duffs and take heed!

Course design is the one aspect of horsemanship that seems to improve on a yearly basis. The only thing course designers and show managers forget from time to time is to bring a natural, country environment to the arena. It often gets too gaudy and artificial. The horses, riders and fences should be on display, not the wings and overabundance of flowers. But it's hard to legislate taste.

After this long evolutionary journey of the last half century, we think it's better and, yet, those who've been around know that a lot has been lost. My generation has had our day. And a great day it was, believe me. Now it's your turn.

Remember, in life the only thing that counts is to try to be the best. There is only one winner. I hope the 21st century will see us back on top on all these fronts, where we belong. We need not accept this rather demoralizing underdog status forever.

18

What Do The "Greats" Have In Common?

June 9, 2000

In order to fall into the category of "great" in any equestrian discipline, one must first of all be a good horseman. And the first mark of a horseman or horsewoman is love of the horse.

Different horsemen feel or express their love of the horse differently. I love, respect, and sympathize with the horse, yet it is not with the same cuddly emotion that I feel for my dogs. Often the greatest riders and trainers are strong and strict with their horses. Tough love! I strongly believe that anyone with a long and successful past-performance record with his horses has a real love for them somewhere.

One cannot reach greatness in our sport, or anything else, without a certain degree of innate talent. Most people in the horse business can become adequate or good, but not *great*. They just do not have enough talent, physically, mentally, emotionally, or a combination of the three. I'm not saying that someone has to have talent of genius proportion to become great. But they do have to possess enough.

The correct word from a teaching perspective for the innate talent is aptitude.

Aptitude and attitude are entirely different. Aptitude has to do with talent; attitude has to do with desire, perseverance, heart, consistency and work ethic. Gordon Wright used to tell us he'd take attitude over aptitude any day of the week. We all know of extremely talented horse people who never got very far.

All the greats that I've ever known have had a burning desire. They eat, sleep and drink horses, horses, horses. They are obsessed and possessed. And because of this desire they have an incredible work ethic. They simply work harder than the others.

People often say about great winners, "He's dumb," or "She's dumb!" Don't believe it! Greats are always smart. They might be smart in different ways, but for sure they are all horse-smart. Most are also street-smart. And some are intellectually smart as well.

The Europeans have a great expression: "He's a winner." "She's a winner." "A certain horse is a winner." Greats are always winners. They're always winning blue ribbons.

Often you can't put your finger on why. But if you really sat down with pen in hand and analyzed it, you'd come up with logical answers. There are a lot of very good riders who win a lot of ribbons, but not a lot of classes. They are not real winners and, therefore, cannot be considered among the real greats.

The greats, in order to win classes, must find and gather good horses. In other words, they must have an "eye" for a horse. Without this, they'll perhaps be great caretakers or good riders, teachers and trainers. But they'll never really make it.

In our business the horse makes the man (or woman) as much or more as the other way around. Again, I've seen so many good people miss out because they don't have an "eye" for a horse. I think it's something some people are just born with, although others certainly can learn it.

The real greats of any era, almost without exception, were great caretakers. Or they surrounded themselves with great caretakers, veterinarians and blacksmiths. Gen. Humberto Mariles, the Mexican gold medalist in 1948, never went far without his trusty veterinarian, "Pallo" Franco.

Liz Edgar, David Broome's sister, one of the great women show jumpers of all time, comes to mind. She and her horses are always perfectly turned out going to the ring. She is a study in the classic, English tradition of proper turn-out. Nick Skelton, another product of the Ted Edgar school, is the same way. His horses still look the best at a show.

Rodrigo and Nelson Pessoa are examples of greats who take care of their horses in a traditional yet modern way. Every new technique concerning management is added to what Nelson already knows regarding stable management. Anne Kursinski does the same.

In any discipline, a horse must be obedient, supple, relaxed and yet still expressive and wanting to do its job. Once the spirit is extinguished from a horse, he might go through the motions, but his brilliance and his ability to perform is dulled. The really great horsemen understand this.

Everybody strives for "round" today, both on the flat and over fences. Very few in the hunter/jumper world understand that "round" means the whole horse: the engagement of the joints of the hind legs, his back, his neck, poll and jaw. Really true roundness is a complex concept to learn.

Each of us is an individual, and we interpret things a bit differently and in our own way. Hans-Günter Winkler and Piero d'Inzeo were totally different in their philosophies and methodologies. Yet they were both enormous winners at the highest level during the 1950s and 1960s.

Some people believe and do things very differently than what I believe and do. Still, I respect and admire them for their consistent success. As Gordon Wright taught us: The important thing is to have a system, believe in a system, and stick to a system. Let the system work for you. Don't change all the time.

Every great jumping rider I've ever known had faith—unshakable faith—in his system. And no matter what the system, it ended up working.

Horses just jump better for some people than others. Rodney Jenkins could get even mediocre horses to jump well. He could get horses to jump with a great bascule—their heads, necks, backs, front ends and hind ends all worked to the best of their ability. Benny O'Meara and Bernie Traurig could to the same thing.

All the greats get horses jumping better, and consistently cleaner, than other riders. Only great riders feel a quality jump on a consistent basis.

In order to be in the great category, one must win the big classes. And to win when it counts, one must show their horses with an intelligent strategy. The greats are smart in when, where and how much they show their horses. You don't see enough "smarts" in show jumping today.

People often ask me how to get to the top. Foremost, it's sacrifice. You must almost give up your life. There is a simple-minded obsession you must possess that is either in you or not. Self-discipline goes without saying. And it's self-discipline on all fronts. I can't underestimate attention to detail. The big things are obvious and easy. It's the little things that are important.

Unfortunately, putting it all together is very tough. That's why when a great one crosses your path, prick your ears and pay attention. It's a rare privilege to watch and bask in the shadow.

May we always have the greats to show us the way.

19

We've Got To Get Our Show
Jumping Out Of Its Rut

February 2, 2001

Yes, we are all disappointed in our show jumping results over the past 10 years. And when I say "all," I mean riders, owners, sponsors and administrators, as well as the general supporters and public.

How can a country with the tradition, history, horsemanship and success of ours have such uneven results in show jumping as we've shown lately?

How can Molly Ashe, Alison Firestone, Katie Monahan Prudent, Beezie Madden, and Peter Wylde sweep the European indoor grand prix circuit, only for us to finish sixth in last year's Olympics, ninth in the 1998 World Equestrian Games, and settle for the silver in the 1999 Pan Am Games? (We used to usually win the Pan Am gold.)

No it's not the fault of the riders, or of the horses. We have had some great riders and horses in these recent championships.

It is the fault of the system. The system is not broken, but it is badly in need of repair.

As a rider, teacher and trainer, it has always been instructive for me to study the past in order to learn for the future. It is important to always review basics, to always review fundamentals.

I've said this so many times before: In many ways we have the greatest system in the world, and riders and trainers from all over the world have learned much from us. Our resources are extraordinary. It amazes me that Brazil can now consistently beat us in Nations Cups and that Canada, without nearly our resources, can be so close (and sometimes they do beat us). What are they doing that we aren't?

Our tradition and history of horsemanship is one of the finest in the world. Through the first half of the 20th century, our cavalry officers trained throughout Europe at the great centers of horsemanship of the day. The knowledge they acquired was brought back to Fort Riley (Kan.) and put together to form our great American style. I'm talking about men like Guy V. Henry and Harry D. Chamberlin, who literally wrote the book on it.

In the second half of the century, the U.S. Equestrian Team so beautifully picked up the ball when the cavalry disbanded, and they began supporting, training and fielding teams to compete all over the world with unparalleled results. Of course, putting Bertalan de Nemethy in the position of chef d'equipe/trainer was just what the doctor ordered and insured our success. He was at the helm for 27 years with undisputed authority and, of course, the results speak for themselves.

For quite a few years after World War II, a small group of well-to-do, cultured and socially prominent men and women ran the horse world as we know it today. They were responsible for the three major institutions—American Horse Shows Association, U.S. Equestrian Team and the National Horse Show (N.Y.). These three institutions, in fact, ran the horse world. Because the same small group headed each organization, there were no disputes and everyone got along quite well.

Now, of course, the business has gotten so big and spread out that totally different people run each of the organizations. That has caused immense friction, especially when there are strong egos and volatile temperaments running the show. I would say the friction started about 15 years ago but really intensified over the past five years.

This fighting amongst ourselves must cease before there is any real chance of our regaining consistent success against our competition abroad. This turmoil has weakened us considerably internationally.

No, we probably can't go back to the de Nemethy era and have a team training center, a team coach, and put the best horses with the best riders. Actually, no country in the world does it exactly that way anymore. That was the U.S. Army way, and those days are over. But we can look at Bert's blueprint and try to adapt—for today's world—from it.

In the beginning (late 1950s-1960), Bert essentially concentrated on four riders. They were to be his riders for the Pan Am games, World Championships and Olympic Games, as well as for Nations Cups and international shows during the year.

During the 1960s, Bert enlarged his focus to probably six to eight riders. And during his last full decade (1970s), he increased it to perhaps eight to 12 riders.

Bert had a wonderful clinic system with the USET. And along with the AHSA Medal Finals and the ASPCA Maclay Finals, these clinics provided Bert with fresh, young talent to bring to the

111

USET headquarters in Gladstone, N.J., for long-term training.

All these stepping stones provided for the proper preparation of horses and riders before selection. My point is that the combination of Gladstone, the American national shows, and European international shows not only showed Bert which were the strongest horse/rider combinations for that year's championship, but they also allowed those horses and riders to be ready when they got there.

With our current system of selection, real preparation is accidental, if at all. We are so consumed with selection we've all but forgotten the important ingredient of the experience you need to have before you get to a championship.

Yes, the 1996 Atlanta Olympic selection process worked out as well as it could have, right down to the 12th horse. We won a silver medal. But that squad—Michael Matz, Anne Kursinski, Leslie Howard and Peter Leone—had tremendous international experience.

The big discussion over the past 12 years has been whether to use an objective or a subjective selection procedure, or a combination of both. My concern as co-chef d'equipe is not so much with how we pick teams as it is with how we prepare them.

Over the past six years, we have really been emphasizing the European tours. There have been a number of USET-sponsored senior tours, developing rider tours, and private tours. All of these tours and trips to European shows do provide experience and preparation leading up to championship, which occur three out of four years. While we should keep this going, our program ensures that it is a little bit by chance whether these will be the same horses and riders who will be on the championship team.

Take the 2000 Olympic team. All were great horses and riders, but few of these partnerships had any depth of international experience. They were up against teams that work as teams on a weekly, monthly, yearly basis all across Europe and around the world. How would you feel being dropped into a situation like Sydney "cold turkey"? It's tough.

"My concern is not so much with how we pick teams as it is with how we prepare them."

We are the only country in the world that uses a totally subjective system to select teams. Canada has part objective and part subjective. England has also tried this method, but I don't think they liked it. Perhaps we need objective, perhaps subjective, or perhaps a combination of the two. I do know that no two people in our show jumping community seem to agree. I also know in light of our resources, we should win more—we should do better, a lot better!

Most other countries hire a chef d'equipe, pay him a big salary, and let him do his job, which is to select, prepare and build teams. Some of these chefs are asked to eliminate their other horse-related activities or any potential conflicts of interest, which is a good idea. Most top horsemen in Europe decline the job, just as they would here in this country. It's a thankless job, hard work if done right, and it can never compensate you enough for the business lost at home.

"It is the fault of the system."

If we care to continue down the road of objective selection through a series of trials, we must consider a few points, the main one being to concentrate on fewer candidates. One must pass through one gate to get to the next. For example, to be eligible for a trial one must have (with the same horse) been in the top six of a grand prix worth $50,000 or more.

By April 1 (approximately), trials or a trial should have narrowed the contestants down to a minimum of 10 and a maximum of 15 contenders. These 10 to 15 horse/rider combinations would have to participate in a European tour during the summer. This should be the much-needed preparation before that year's championship.

The final team would be selected from a short, final trial after all the tours were completed. Believe me, this would not be too much jumping, providing the riders use good, common sense horsemanship before and during their show season. People have a misconception about our trials and the amount of jumping a horse has to do. A successful horse at Aachen (Germany) finishes the show after having jumped seven or eight big rounds.

We must also try to raise the bar on our national front. One thing that helped keep us so strong years ago was our fall indoor circuit. Up through the mid-1980s, our indoor shows were as strong as anywhere in the world. Now, for a variety of reasons (the latest being the West Nile virus) the level of our international competition at these shows has really declined. I doubt we can ever really bring this back to the standard we had years ago. So let's concentrate on developing really good outdoor CSIOs and CSIs, run first class, and offering big prize money. If possible, we've got to get the "big boys" from Europe coming to us, instead of us always going to them.

Yes, it is discouraging to ride the show jumping roller coaster now in this country. But at least we are having some highs, and we know we've got the resources with the owners, horses and riders. That is a positive.

It is time to attack on all these fronts. First, let's all start working together and get this AHSA/USET mess behind us and get going forward. Second, we must become logical in our ways of selecting and preparing teams so the right team has a good fighting chance of winning on the right day. It is more, much more, than selection; it is preparation and winning. And third, we must raise our national standards, which really prepare people and horses to compete internationally and eventually to be part of winning championships teams.

It is the next, younger generation's turn to govern and get these things done. 🐎

20

Where Did We Come From? Where Are We Going?

July 7, 2006

There are very few horsemen (or horsewomen) that I would consider "genius." Jack Le Goff is one of those rare few—Olympic rider, teacher, trainer, theoretician, coach and, now, author.

When talking to Jack the other day about his new book, I asked him what was wrong. He hit the nail on the head, as usual: The young trainers are teaching their students to *compete*. They are not, necessarily, teaching them to *ride*.

Jack elaborated a bit further: Therefore, when the student reaches a certain level, he or she fails or falls short. The student doesn't really know how to ride.

It all starts—riding that is—with one's own self-sufficiency with one's horse. Do you know what he eats? How to bed a stall? How to clean a stall? How to properly lead a horse, groom a horse, trim or clip a horse? Do you know all about tack, bitting and how to keep your equipment scrupulously clean? Do you know how to load and ship a horse? Do you know how to polish your boots the night before you ride? Have you ridden all different kinds of horses, with all kinds of problems? Have you produced green horses?

These are just some of the many things that come way before competing with a horse. These are the basics, the platform from which you might successfully and correctly reach the top of your particular discipline.

I witness great disappointment time and time again in America when a rider fails to reach the top. He or she can't quite make it. After all, the parents have sacrificed enormously in time, money and effort. The trainer and pupil have worked long, hard hours together on position, flatwork and jumping courses.

And, yet, the "Peter Principle" rears its ugly head. (The original principle states that in a hierarchically structured administration, people tend to be promoted up to their "level of incompetence.") Far too soon, the whole project falls short. Whether it's to the top end of the hunter division, the Medal Finals, grand prix, or the Olympic Games, it doesn't matter. The horsemanship is not there, the attention to detail is not there, the spit and polish is not there, the practiced toughness is not there, the experience garnered from thousands of problems is not there.

No matter how much money is spent and no matter how fabulous the horses, it's truly inconceivable to compete against, let alone beat, the true professional horsemen of the sport without this built-in experience, without this toughness of character.

In the earlier days of my teaching—a different time, a different place and a different culture—young people sought true horsemanship. They wanted problems. They wanted a myriad of experiences with horses, often not easy or pleasant. The good teachers had time to accommodate this indispensable part of

117

the sport.

Time and space and competition have encroached on our wonderful sport of riding and jumping horses. Everyone is rushing. One cannot rush with horses. It's literally the "kiss of death." Even our top team riders are all over the map trying to do too many things at once.

Space has curtailed the natural aspects of our sport. Rings, be they for hunters or jumpers, are constantly being reduced in size. As a consequence, collection is over-emphasized and jump construction is becoming more artificial. The *sine qua non* (essential meaning) of course building for the hunters or the jumpers is to bring the country to the arena. Miniature golf is not what the sport is all about. That's why I still love to go to Hickstead, England.

All over the world, there are too many horse shows. Horse shows in all disciplines are taking over the sport. Trainers like horse shows (and I've been a trainer, believe me) because it's good business. Day money. Riders like horse shows because of their egos. Horse show managers like horse shows because of money. It all goes back to dollars, cents and egos.

No. That's not the real point. As Robert Dover has said, "It's the journey that counts. Blue ribbons are a dime a dozen. If you're smart, it's not difficult to win at horse shows, any horse show. What gives real pleasure and value is getting to the horse show."

We used to be at horse shows about 20 percent of the time. Most of the time, we were at home with our horses, taking care of them, going cross-country, taking lessons, riding on our own, and figuring things out.

Now, many people are at horse shows 80 percent of the time. Showing, showing, showing. If you're a true horseman, you know

118

that is not true value. The physical, mental, emotional and spiritual connection with the horse cannot be the same under the constant stress. Yes, that adrenaline rush is important to experience from time to time, but not on a weekly, let alone daily, basis. It's not healthy for man or beast.

It's exactly the same in going to school. Homework (practice) supplements class and lecture time (lessons). All of this work prepares for tests (horse shows). Horse shows are simply a barometer, a test of where you stand relative to your peers in the art of riding and jumping.

During the last year, I've experienced three events—a small indoor show in Germany (actually only a half-hour from Aachen), a clinic in St. Petersburg, Russia, and a clinic in Hungary—which made me not only appreciate, but actually worship, the principles of Caprilli, Santini, Chamberlin, Gordon Wright, Jimmy Williams, Vladimir Littauer, Jack Le Goff, as well as other advocates of the forward seat more than ever.

Violating these precious principles not only makes for insecure, unbalanced, inefficient and ugly riding, but also for disturbed horses performing badly. It's usually the misinterpretation and/or exaggeration of a technique that causes things to go badly astray.

Dressage, well done, can be a wonderful thing. Dressage, however, can be a risky venture

"In the earlier days of my teaching, young people sought true horsemanship."

"Everyone is rushing. One cannot rush with horses. It's literally the 'kiss of death.'"

for those who want to gallop and jump horses, especially the way it's practiced today with very long stirrups, loose lower legs, riders excessively behind the motion and horses over-collected and over-flexed. Littauer and others warned us 50 years ago of this possibility, and he was right. I'm sure he would be shaking his finger at all the hoop-la over Rollkur!

What I have witnessed, perhaps most apparently in Eastern Europe, but also in other parts of the world, are classic violations of a correct position for riding and jumping. The repercussions of incorrect riding take their toll on the rider but, worse still, the horse!

First, the stirrups are often too long, undermining the support for the rider. (By the way, all of these funny, new-fangled stirrups being sold do nothing to help. They are a detriment.) Stirrups too long, especially for galloping and jumping, are infinitely worse than stirrups too short. One must reach for the stirrup, and it destabilizes the leg, making it impossible to close the angles of the ankle, knee and hip.

With these long stirrups, the heels come up, further loosening the leg, as well as promoting an unauthorized active leg, driving and irritating the horse by mistake. This, in turn, makes for a clash of aids that deadens the sides and mouth of the horse.

These riders have been taught to lean back to such an extent that most of their weight (if not all) is on the buttocks. The weight should be distributed between crotch, seat bones, heels and stirrups.

As a result of this faulty weight distribution, the rider is given a rough ride. He has to constantly catch up with his horse, which causes excess upper body motion, acrobatics, and gyrations, plus the fact that the tender loins of the horse are abused and become sore, as well as defensive. No wonder there are so many back problems in the horse world today, for both horse and rider.

Because the upper body doesn't shift to the front in various degrees at the different gaits, especially posting, galloping and jumping, posture is compromised drastically, characterized by roached backs and leading with the head and shoulders.

Staying with the motion, or center of gravity, is totally foreign to this *backward* way of riding.

Most of the riders I watched or taught looked down far too much. Like it does while driving a car, this habit directly affects the coordination of aids, control, balance and security.

Violating the great principle of a straight line from elbow to the horse's mouth always has repercussions. Stargazing and head tossing will be only some of the resistances encountered. Human nature will always try to "pull" the horse's head back down rather than "push" it down. Higher hands, closed fingers, straight wrists, and thumbs just inside the vertical are secrets to putting a good mouth on a horse.

Believe me, basic principles and theories that are often being taught in other parts of the world are far from what we've always been taught as correct equitation.

It's interesting from a teacher's perspective to see this, work with it, and try to help and enlighten people in other parts of the world. And, believe me, you're certainly doing the horse a favor to stop irritating his rib cage, get off his back and have great consideration for his mouth. Good teaching, as well as good all-around horsemanship, is all about the horse. The rider is just the conduit.

What Good Teachers Teach

Tricia Booker photo

21

The Importance Of
Natural Obstacles

April 6, 1990

Remembering the fundamentals and where we came from is always important. The hunter, jumper and hunter seat equitation divisions derived from the hunting field. They began as contests to determine the best horse or rider galloping over uneven terrain and jumping natural obstacles.

Today we are so removed from the starting point that in some cases it's sad. Many horse show participants—managers, judges, course designers, owners, riders or trainers—know so little and care less about the starting point of this sport of show ring riding and jumping that they profess to love so much.

I think this is terribly wrong. We should, whenever possible, stay close to the natural beginnings of our show ring sport.

Artificiality in showing has reached an acute stage in the hunter division, more so than in the equitation or jumper division. I well remember the days of the Greenwich, Ox Ridge, Fairfield, North Shore and Piping Rock outside courses. They were long, galloping courses over big, solid, natural hedges, walls, post-and-rails, coops, millbrooks, aikens and snake fences.

While ditches and banks weren't the norm for show hunters, they were occasionally to be found. Devon's outside course presented a log fence with a ditch on the landing side and a table bank to be jumped back in to the main ring.

The fences in those days were so far apart they were unrelated. There was no need to know or count strides. It was a question of pace and meeting your fences "on the fly."

Unfortunately, today's horse shows don't have time for these courses. There is so much of everything—divisions, classes, horses and people. A true outside course at most of today's shows wouldn't be feasible.

And, god forbid, a natural ditch or bank! These hot-house flowers (horses and riders) would have a nervous breakdown, cry at the in-gate, and probably refuse to show.

Many of today's hunter riders—and unfortunately their horses—would freak out if they saw what had to be jumped up hill and down dale at the old Michigan summer circuit. That was what gallop and jump was meant to be. How did we lose it?

I'm not just singling out the hunter division when it comes to natural fences, proper courses, and a most limited American mentality. The jumper division is basically in the same boat.

An example is the magnificent new Palm Beach (Fla.) Equestrian Center—and this is the way it is at 95 percent of our jumper shows. The ring is superb—a big grass field, perfect footing, in a gorgeous amphitheater setting. They've had it almost two years now, and still there isn't one natural fence.

The only two major shows that I attend on the East Coast that have really made an effort toward building fences are Old Salem and Southampton, both in New York. I've designed rings and built fences at the old Palm Beach and Lake Placid, only to have the managers over the years eliminate one jump at a time because they are a maintenance problem and "in the way."

There can be many permanent fences—walls, hedges and even gates are a must. A big mistake many shows make is to have only a big 12-foot open water. That's the quickest way to ruin young horses and give them a water problem forever. Always prepare horses by giving them single and double liverpools 4 to 6 feet wide. To be really correct, have a 10-foot open water available to get horses really confident.

I like dry ditches too, 4 to 6 feet wide. It's important to have these ditches at different depths, from 6 inches to several feet is a good range.

A devil's dike or Pulverman's grob add more variety to the ditch concept.

There are many, many types of banks. For show jumpers I like the wide table banks with one or two strides, or big slide banks. I don't like the bounce-type of Irish bank because it can teach horses to stick their feet down in to big hedges built in to oxers or triple bars. We must remember these are show jumpers, not event horses.

One's own imagination and experience can provide many combinations of these obstacles or design new ones. I love a variety as long as it's not artificial or gimmicky.

"Artificiality in showing has reached an acute stage in the hunter division, more so than in the equitation or jumper division."

"And, god forbid, a natural ditch or bank! These hot-house flowers (horses and riders) would have a nervous breakdown."

Natural obstacles are so very important because they advance a horse's and a rider's boldness. When one advances in boldness, there is an increase in scope—the ability to jump wider, though not necessarily higher.

My grand prix training field at Hunterdon is full of natural jumps. And all of my spring and summer schooling sessions center on training over these types of fences. Horses grow up faster, become braver and more relaxed, and in the end learn to jump bigger courses.

I also never have to worry about going to any show in the world. My horses have been to a comprehensive school and are prepared. For this reason there is nothing better for a young grand prix horses' or riders' education than to take a trip outside the United States. They see nothing but a constant variety of natural fences and come home so much wiser and braver.

Let's not leave this tried-and-true training advantage to others. Let's do it ourselves, for our own good, by putting some natural jumps in all our rings.

22

Teaching With The Grading System

May 4, 1990

All good instruction, be it in school or on horseback, is progressive. My great mentor, the late Gordon Wright, followed this grading system way back when most of us were still groping in the dark trying to get our heels down.

He always told us we'd reached the third grade after he'd given us 50 hours of instruction. Now, after having taught many years myself, I guess he was about right.

Riding solo, though, is the name of the game. And our whole idea during the course of instruction from beginning to end is to provide the student with self-sufficiency and independence.

We really want to develop as complete a horseperson as possible. They should learn to deal with colts, ride across country, foxhunt, perhaps gallop a race horse or compete in dressage. These are all equally important building blocks toward creating the complete horseman or horsewoman.

Let's begin with kindergarten or first grade—someone's first few times on a horse. As a teacher I want *total* control, so I keep my pupil on the lead line or longe line. Then, if anything goes wrong I can physically control the horse.

The student is just out of the womb, so to speak, and is a helpless victim to even the tiniest misdemeanor.

The vehicle for first grade work should be a foolproof school horse, absolutely dog quiet. If this horse cannot tolerate his rider carrying and probably using a short stick, then he's too hot.

I never teach nor allow people to kick—it's a bad habit. A stick replaces kicking. If someone is already a kicker, a stick is the correct substitute.

All I want at this very first stage of riding are the basic mechanics of position and control. These include the four parts of the rider's body (legs, base, upper body, head and arms), equilibrium, eyes, how to apply the brakes (first), how to apply the gas (second), and steering with an opening rein. The rider must not be overmounted or overfaced as both produce physical and mental fear and prevent the rider from concentrating on what he's doing on a horse.

We wean our pupil as soon as possible from being dependent on our physical connection via the longe line. For me as a beginning rider, this was a very, very big step. I was so terrified when starting to ride that Miss Townsend and her assistant, Nancy Moran, had to keep me at their side on a line a whole winter at the Ox Ridge Hunt Club.

The grades advance and so do the problems. It's not enough to teach people how to ride. As a horseman and a teacher, I must inspire my charges to learn about other things besides riding: building a facility, stable management, shoeing, veterinary care, shipping, course building, and much more.

In the old days we learned and enjoyed doing it all. That's the way it was done then. Now it's too specialized and the pupil is much too dependent on his support system—his trainer, groom, veterinarian, blacksmith, van driver, and a cast of thousands.

We've all become soft and reliant, and I include myself. The difference, though, is that people of my generation have done it, and we could do it again in a pinch. Many of today's young people simply can't—and it's not their fault, it's their teachers'.

"The idea, teachers, is to teach your students your craft and gradually, silently, invisibly move away. I don't see this happening today."

The idea, teachers, is to teach your students your craft and gradually, silently, invisibly move away. I don't see this happening today, and I understand why.

These are not just students; they are show ring stars, clients, big accounts. Just from a dollars-and-cents point of view, it's hard to let go. But let go to a certain degree with each and every year you must.

My experience has taught me that the more you are willing to let go of a student as he progresses from grade to grade, the longer lasting is the relationship. I have "lost" very few people adhering to this principle. They almost always come back in one way or another. I'm teaching people today I worked with 25 years ago, and sometimes I'm teaching their children.

"Our whole idea during the course of instruction is to provide the student with self-sufficiency and independence."

Advanced Medal/Maclay work is comparable to high school, grand prix riding is comparable to college, and being a professional or Olympian is equal to post-graduate work. To see men and women in this grade of riding being spoon-fed is really wrong.

It's wrong because we're not forcing them out in to the world on their own two feet. And without this opportunity to stand tall and make their own mistakes, how can we expect them to become master horsemen, teachers, trainers and professionals in their own right? All we're doing is shortchanging our future generations of American horsemen.

We have a great tradition in this country of equitation. It's sympathetic, light, soft, strong, practical and intelligent. There isn't much we can't do with our horses and riders in most any discipline that isn't better than most people in other countries. Let's preserve it!

Follow the grading system. And remember your only job is to provide the thinking, intelligent, comprehensive horsemen and horsewomen of the future. 🐎

23

Closing The Angles

August 3, 1990

Watching some of today's instructors can be alarming, whether they're teaching younger children, adult amateurs or dressage. Unfortunately, judges follow and pin what's being taught, and teachers teach what judges like, so we end up in a vicious circle.

Teaching riding and judging riders, be it hunter seat equitation or dressage, is relatively easy if you understand the mechanics. By the mechanics, I mean the angles, just like the ones you evaluate on a horse. Angles make it black and white.

The first angle in riding is the ankle angle, between the foot and the shin. How do we create this angle? First, by adjusting the stirrups correctly in accordance with what we're doing on the horse.

This is easy for the mounted rider to do by himself, even without an instructor. Take your feet out of the stirrups and really stretch your legs straight down. Where does the stirrup iron hit your foot or leg in relation to the ankle bone? For dressage and flatwork for hunters, jumpers or equitation, it should be just below the ankle.

In my opinion, dressage riders worldwide are riding too long. I much preferred the style in the dressage ring years ago to what I see today, especially the short women reaching for their stirrups, sometimes barely able to keep them on their feet.

While jumping low fences up to 3'6", a good rule of thumb is for the stirrup to hit the bottom of the ankle bone. For every foot you jump higher, shorten up a good hole. For puissance and grand prix classes, the stirrup should be just above the ankle.

Racing, of course, is the opposite of dressage, as the iron will hit far up the rider's leg.

How else do we ensure that this angle remains closed? Simply by keeping the heels lower than the toes. This is important, for when the toe is carried up and the heel weighted down, a certain tension is produced in the calf muscles, which provides the rider with a strong and secure lower leg. Once the toe is lower than the heel, a certain slackness comes into the calf muscles. The legs are no lighter tight, secure or strong. Slack legs are useless; tight legs are powerful.

Working on up the rider's body, we come to the knee angle, formed by the back of the calf and the back of the thigh. Again, I first produce the knee's angle I want by adjusting the stirrups.

For a more open knee angle (dressage, saddle seat, or stock seat), the stirrups are a bit longer. For jumping the stirrups naturally come up a bit.

The legs also must be in position, just behind the girth. If the legs shoot forward, the knee angle will open up. Teachers must correct this and judges must penalize it.

The rider's base of support (seat and thighs) must also be adjusted properly to the front-center of the saddle, not back toward the cantle. The rider must sit "over" his legs, not "behind" them.

If the legs and seat are in the right position, and the stirrups are the correct length, the angle at the knee will correctly fall in to place.

During all the sitting work, this knee angle stays closed; for posting galloping and jumping, it opens and closes from the movement and thrust of the horse.

The rider doesn't do it, the horse does!

"Why do many instructors tell their beginners to 'sit up and lean back'?"

The third angle is the hip angle, formed at the pelvic region between the top of the thigh and the rider's torso. The rider must consciously at first, and then automatically, open and close the angle.

Stirrup length has little to do with this angle, although a shorter stirrup for galloping and jumping provides support for the feet and makes it easier for the rider to stand up and lean forward.

Many people today have forgotten or are confused about when and where this angle should open or close. For "with the motion" riding, the hip angle yearns to close; for "behind the motion" riding (dressage, saddle seat, stock seat), the angle wants to remain quite open.

"Just understand the angles, and everything will fall into place."

Let's begin at the halt: The hip angle closes just a few degrees; the upper body is ever so slightly in front of the vertical to accompany the horse's movement. The sitting trot and canter have the same position and angulation.

For posting, galloping and jumping, the hip angle closes up to 30 degrees in front of the perpendicular. This is because as we rise out of the saddle, we must lean forward to keep with the horse's movement easily and efficiently.

Only for extreme emergencies necessitating tremendous drive, restraint or balance do we lean back. Why, then, do many of today's instructors tell their beginners to sit up and lean back?

For some, it's making life harder because they have to duck over to catch up. For others, its making it nearly impossible as they get left behind, jump ahead, or even fall off.

Teachers, go back and read the forward seat literature to learn the truth, American literature by American authors such as Harry D. Chamberlin, Gordon Wright, Vladimir Littauer and myself.

The fourth angle, which riders of every discipline need to understand, is the elbow angle created by the forearm and upper arm. This angle is automatically and correctly produced when there is a straight line between the rider's elbow and the horse's mouth. If the horse is a bit high-headed, the hands will follow suit and be a bit higher. The opposite is also true.

When riding with a broken line above the mouth, this angle will close too much; a broken line below the mouth will open the angle too much. While riding above and below the mouth is not always wrong, and we should all know how to do it, the better daily practice is a straight line.

A broken line below the mouth and too open an angle is especially damaging as the hands become heavier and shoulders and backs easily become rounded.

Forget the complicated things for the moment. It's the simple things that are important. By adhering to the fundamentals, you produce the classic, beautiful, functioning rider that we in this country are known for.

Just understand angles, and everything will fall into place.

135

24

Gordon Wright's 12 Commandments Of A Teacher

October 5, 1990

Gordon Wright, my mentor and teacher, wrote out 12 commandments at one of the last teaching clinics we did together, giving explanations and examples as he did. Now I'll give a brief explanation of them with my own interpretation. They are things all of us who teach must constantly review.

1. Know your subject. You must never attempt to teach something you don't really know. And if you don't know about it, don't pretend. Some teachers have never experienced something firsthand. They can still understand and teach through what others have done and through reading.

From the pupil's point of view it's a stronger argument if the teacher can, or at one time could, do what he's asking the student to do. The problem today is that many people "parrot" information. They haven't really studied in depth what they're talking about. I suggest reading.

2. Seek to create development in each student. Everyone

has a different physical and mental make-up, different goals, and varying degrees of talent. All of these factors should be taken into account in bringing people along.

But today it's all show, show, show. Not everybody is meant to show, or event or jump. Their physical and mental ability gets in the way. There is foxhunting, dressage, teaching, green horses to make, and lots of other things to do with horses. Point your students toward what they would do best. One in 100,000 students jumps a fence like Conrad Homfeld or Katie Prudent.

3. Look for new experiences and problems. This commandment is definitely not adhered to enough in the horse show world today: same routine day after day, week after week, year after year. That's why we're not producing the well-rounded horsemen, horsewomen and the great riders of several decades ago.

These people were brought up to cope with everything and to ride everything—green and rough horses included. They foxhunted and they galloped race horses. They even rode races. Nowadays, immersed in a soft, self-satisfied society, teachers and trainers seek to avoid problems for pampered students, hoping not to rock the boat.

That is wrong! Weak riders are the result.

4. Avoid sarcasm and never ridicule a pupil. This has always been a tough one for me, and for Gordon Wright. And for all the great teachers I've been with or watched. It's a matter of timing. Sometimes people need to be shaken up. Then they can do more than they think they can.

Let's face it, some trainers can get away with anything and everybody loves them. Others cannot. It's a question of personality. Personality, charm and flair separate the "good" from the "great."

5. Be enthusiastic about learning.
Enthusiasm makes the difference. Probably no other factor is as important in teaching as enthusiasm. It can override a multitude of sins. Think of the people you've known who couldn't ride and didn't even know how to mount. Yet they were successful teachers. Do you know why? They were enthusiastic.

There is nothing worse than a dull, boring, negative teaching personality. You can see it in teaching the simplest things—how to stop a horse, or how to do a shoulder-in, for example.

6. Instill confidence.
From the rider's (and the horse's) point of view, nothing beats confidence. A lesson or a schooling session is always a game—to stretch the confidence level but never to break it. Once confidence is lost, you have to go back—sometimes way back—and build it up again.

Instilling confidence is quite an art in teaching or training. In order to develop the horse or rider, there must be a constant stretch, often almost to the breaking point. That's how you get maiden equitation riders to the Olympic Games.

I'm going to stop now. For those dedicated to teaching, six commandments are enough to read, digest and really apply in their daily work.

The best teaching and training methods revolve around one thing at a time, or at most a very few things at a time. Think hard.

"The problem today is that many people haven't really studied in-depth what they're talking about."

"The best teaching and training methods involve one thing at a time."

138

Gordon Wright wrote the headings to this outline, and I always paid particular attention when he spoke.

25

The Twelve Commandments Of A Teacher—Continued

November 2, 1990

In the previous column, I reviewed the first six of Gordon Wright's 12 commandments of a teacher. This month I'll continue with my interpretation of the second six of Gordon's commandments.

7. Prevent physical fear since it is impossible to learn with it. This is an especially important commandment to remember when working with beginners, timid riders or adults. Accidents are counterproductive. Not only do people get hurt, but people's concentration also all but disappears when they're afraid of getting hurt. Physical fear is a lot more serious than mental fear, the fear of making a mistake.

But, as with all the commandments, you don't have to go overboard. America has become a soft society. We have almost a paranoia when it comes to safety and protection. As riders grow, they must experience "blood and guts." It's good for them.

8. Simplify words and actions. This is hard for all of us, but remember the axiom KISS—Keep It Simple, Stupid. Teachers, go to horse shows and listen in the warm-up ring, which has become ludicrous. I often think how lucky I am not to have a trainer. Even with my experience, I couldn't begin to follow some of these complex instructions. A good exercise for every teacher is to take one simple thing and teach it in a very simple way.

9. Don't be a perfectionist, because it's difficult for most students to live with. This is another tough one for me. Being a perfectionist has been my vice and virtue. Fortunately, I've always had a sixth sense that tells me when to let something go. You've got to develop that sixth sense to know when enough of one thing is enough, otherwise mannered, artificial and— worst of all—stiff riders will result.

On the other hand, people who lack a bit of perfectionism in their make-up are usually a bit sloppy and lazy and rarely go to the top. I would rather temper a perfectionist than try to encourage a slob.

10. Demonstrate and teach, thus inspiring pupils to make continual progress. The great teachers I rode with were not just great riding instructors. They set an example in everything they did and were great trainers as well.

Students invariably copy. Every barn has a stamp—whether it be riding apparel, work on the flat, or style over fences—there is a motif. The stamp that I received—from Gordon Wright, Bert de Nemethy and Gunnar Anderson—should be passed on to my pupils. People are followers; they need leaders. The problem is, people today have let their standards drop. The professionals won't suffer from this as much as their protégés.

11. Be especially aware of appearance while riding. This is where standards come in. When a horse and a rider are properly turned out leaving the barn, everything else will fall in to place. It's a question of discipline and effort. If you cut corners grooming a horse, you'll probably cut corners training the horse. It sets the tone for the day.

People laugh because I always wear boots and breeches and insist my students do too. Why? First, all my great mentors always wore boots and breeches, and they were pretty successful. Second, people ride better with boots and breeches. They are less sloppy and, therefore, ride a little bit better. Third, it looks better, just as white will always look better on the tennis court. Don't forget, it's the little details in creating the masterpiece, not the big, obvious things.

12. Have a specific, daily lesson plan. The old pros do this automatically, whether consciously or unconsciously. The younger teacher should probably write it down in outline form. You can't be too organized.

I'm a firm believer in being organized, even over-organized. I believe in knowing what you want to work on ahead of time. Know what your pupil needs to work on that day and have exercises ready. There should be a progressive and logical sequence to every lesson. One thing should lead to another, with a beginning, a middle and an end. A lesson or a schooling session is a creation, nothing less. It is very important.

These are some very good teaching commandments. They have held me in good stead for years and years. Abide by them and

142

I guarantee you success. Keep reviewing, reading, watching, listening and learning.

And don't forget, teachers, you are making people, not just riders. It is the characteristic of the students you produce, not just their records, that count the most.

26

Preparing For The Finals

November 30, 1990

As a result of watching the AHSA Medal Finals at Harrisburg and judging the ASPCA Maclay Finals at the National Horse Show, I felt preparation in the following areas was lacking in about 80 percent of the riders:

–Caring, knowing and really, thoroughly training their own horses to cope with any test that might be presented.

–Position is not what it was. Between the toe being on the stirrup, heels up, too much weight in the buttocks instead of the crotch, upper bodies behind the motion (and sometimes behind the vertical), crest release that is either overdone or not done correctly, and broken lines above or below the horse's mouth, many riders' positions were far from classical.

Whatever happened to jumping out of hand? Once position as we know it to be right is lost, our standards of professional hunter/ jumper riding will deteriorate rapidly. Watch the generation of professionals in their 30s and 40s: Hap Hansen, Ian Millar, Joe Fargis, Michael Matz, Katie Monahan Prudent, Anne Kursinski all have position. Watch them ride.

The psychological preparation of our riders needs work. They appear soft, passive and weak under stress. Train them to have the guts to take a chance. After all, that's what life is all about, and the finals are a wonderful place to learn to "go for it."

Hunter seat equitation is a division unto itself. It is not the hunter division, the jumper division, and most certainly not the dressage division. It was designed to give the young rider the advantage, although that advantage shouldn't necessarily go to the one with the most expensive horse. The emphasis is to encourage all-around riding ability and general horsemanship, not simply to pilot a fancy hunter around and find eight jumps.

This particular division, spelled out loud and clear in all its details in the AHSA Rule Book, probably has been the single most important component in the making of our great international and Olympic riders. No country in the world can boast the countless numbers if jumping stylists that we've been able to produce over the past half a century.

The best way for the layman, rider or trainer alike to understand hunter seat equitation is to really study and learn the rule book. It is always best when participating, coaching or judging to go by the rules to the letter and to know the rules backward and forward. Our hunter seat section is most explicit and clear in describing purpose, position at different gaits, class routine, course requirements, and tests.

Those who are sharp would have even found the word "liverpool" in this section of the book! I am referring to the liverpool in my Maclay Finals course that had such an influence on the outcome of the class.

It always amazes me when trainers, riders and parents,

caught with their pants down so to speak, moan and groan about certain fences or tests after they've been forewarned by the rules that govern the class. Mounting and dismounting, changing horses without outside assistance, and jumping strangely colored walls, small ditches and bounces are not only excellent tests of horsemanship but can also be predicted before you enter the class.

"Once position as we know it to be is lost, our standards will deteriorate quickly."

Once you really—I mean really—study and understand the rules of the game, preparation is at hand. The best preparation for this division is a comprehensive, in-depth education of the rider (and the horse). Ideally, the young rider should have knowledge and some hands-on experience in stable management, course construction, breaking and riding green horses, cross-country riding or foxhunting, flatwork (elementary dressage), gymnastics, jumping, and the elementary showing of hunters and jumpers. If they can also get to gallop a racehorse, work a Saddlebred, sit on a cutting horse, and travel abroad to watch and learn, so much the better.

"A variety of problems is what produces depth and strength."

The point I'm trying to make is that in preparing for the finals, which are after all the national championships, the less limited the better. Usually the young boys and girls with the most practical experience under their breeches come out on top.

Some of the things that I insisted on when I was teaching equitation riders proved invaluable

146

when we reached the end of the year and the finals. I've always asked my staff—excellent horsemen and horsewomen in their own right—to encourage, urge, and if necessary insist on some rider participation around the barn.

Whenever I change the fences in the ring or the grand prix field, I like my riders with me. Slow work, which includes the history, theory and fundamentals of riding, has always been most important to me.

I always supplemented my lesson program with short dressage clinics given by experts that I liked and believed in, including Jessica Ransehausen, Gunnar Andersen, Jack Le Goff, Jean Froissard, Gunnar Ostergaard and Robert Dover. We'd also go cross-country on rigorous rides for an hour or so *without* stirrups.

The equitation riders would school, and sometimes even show, their own made horses and "greenies," both hunters and jumpers. In the old days I'd take my stronger, better kids to horse dealers and put them on 10 or 12 horses a day before going to Harrisburg for the AHSA Medal Finals.

In other words, the preparation was designed to be as comprehensive as possible. A variety of problems is what produces depth and strength.

Finals, championships, Olympic trials and other special days are all pressure situations. In preparing riders, I condition them to pressure. I am a pressure teacher for that very reason. You must practice pressure like everything else, get used to it and be able to handle it. Otherwise there is no hope when that big day comes.

27

What Clinics Should And Shouldn't Be

January 10, 1992

All over the world, clinics are the thing to do today. In all aspects of the sport—from farriers, to veterinarians, to stable management, to riding and driving—clinics are in vogue.

I remember back in the '50s when Gordon Wright, Vladimir Littauer and possibly one or two other hunter/jumper trainers gave an occasional clinic. It was rather unusual.

Gordon Wright started me on the clinic trail back in the early '60s in Beaumont, Texas, and Atlanta. Many people thought clinics were a bad idea: They were short, they confused people and might ruin horses, and who would follow up after the clinic? There were a million reasons why the clinic system of teaching was a risk and was bound to fail.

I vehemently disagreed and stuck to my guns. Yes, clinics are short. No, a good horseman will not ruin horses and riders. The teachers and trainers attending or riding in the clinic will follow up and teach the new techniques they have been taught, I said.

And all of this has come to pass. Clinics have better helped people to manage, ride, drive, and jump their horses in many countries around the world. Clinics are a wonderful thing.

I have had some wonderful people teach at my farm because I'm extremely selective about whom I invite. I don't believe in a clinic for the sake of a clinic. There must be something specific I want my riders to experience and accomplish. Usually it's to acquire better technique in a certain area, such as flatwork or dressage.

Sometimes I want them to be under the spell of a personality like Bert de Nemethy or Jack Le Goff while gaining knowledge. A teacher's mental approach or aura is often just as important as the information he or she can impart. I will never forget the way my great trainers taught me different things.

I also try to be highly selective when I'm invited to give a clinic. Is it an organized situation run by nice people who really care? Or are they a bunch of flakes who just want something to do or want just to have my name at their farm and are in it for all the wrong reasons?

In my earlier days I had a couple of unpleasant experiences staying with people. Now, with just a few exceptions, I stay in a motel.

A good clinic must be perfectly organized by both the host and the clinician. Some of the points to consider are: Meeting the clinician at the airport on time; decent accommodations (luxury not needed); dinner provided for the clinician, but not necessarily with an exhausting social schedule after the clinic; neat and tidy riding areas and barns, although a showplace facility isn't needed; a workmanlike array of jumps; an insistence on punctuality and discipline, because riding is a dangerous sport; a uniform group of riders and horses; a maximum of six to eight hours of teaching per day; well turned-out and well prepared horses and riders.

How much can a horse and rider do in just a couple of days? Not much. I, therefore, explain that it's not how much we do but how much we learn. And, most importantly, how much can the rider apply it to his or her own riding and training?

Often clinicians want to entertain and do too much while teaching very little. Other clinicians are the opposite—they teach too much, talk too much, and let the riders experience too little. A happy medium is best.

Yes, teach new things. But review old things too. You can teach old, simple basics again and again because that's what riders and their horses really need, but do it in different, interesting and fun ways.

Remember to never scare a horse or rider, but don't bore them either. To be dull is to be bad. I believe in simplicity, in doing one thing at a time. Try to simplify your actions and deeds. To teach a simple thing well is often difficult.

It's most important to be progressive in a clinic. Start out easy and end up hard. You don't know what you've got the first day, which is sometimes the only day, so don't get in trouble. On the second day, build on what you did the first day and add some new things. On the third day, even if it's a four or five day clinic, review what you've done.

It's most important at the end of a three-day cycle to consolidate. I usually jump a course, or parts of one, on the third day while concentrating on the basics—position, legs, hands, eyes and striding. In this way we're not just working over a course of jumps, but we're doing it constructively and improving form.

The purpose of a clinic is definitely not to destroy. It's meant to add to a horse's and rider's repertoire. Of course, some people are thin-skinned and will feel torn down. More often than not, that's their problem.

A good teacher will lose one student by being a disciplinarian, but 10 more will follow. People want discipline. They know it's right, and they know it's for their own good.

The purpose of a clinic is *not* to buy and sell horses. Some famous show riders give clinics only for that reason, and it's unfair. Fortunately, most people can see right through this type of clinician. I admit I've seen some good horses in clinics and transactions have transpired, but that's not why I was there.

"To be dull is to be bad. To teach a simple thing well is often difficult."

Extra lecture sessions, questions and answers, and videotape viewing are all wonderful in theory. But after eight hours everyone is exhausted, and I don't think anyone can concentrate, so I discourage these sessions because I don't think they are beneficial.

Giving clinics is a business just like other aspects of the horse business. There is no free lunch. And if it is free, people should pay something anyway and donate it to some worthy organization. It's human nature that people get much more out of the things they pay for.

"I don't believe in a clinic for the sake of a clinic."

I ask for one check from the organizer, not a bunch of checks from people I don't know, to cover all my expenses, riders' fees and spectators' fees. Spectators are there for one reason—to learn. And they should pay for that, otherwise they shouldn't be there. 🐎

28

Get Out Of The Ring!

July 9, 1993

I know I've said this before, but it must be said again and again, perhaps even more strongly for the benefit of horse show managers, trainers, exhibitors and even judges and course designers.

Much of our horsemanship has become so very limited, weak, artificial and affected. And there is one reason: We have become ring-bound, which is the same as people who mentally or physically become house-bound.

Several weeks ago I took some students to a one-day show at Judy Richter's Coker Farm in New York. This was a fun show that felt a bit old-fashioned, which wasn't at all bad. The jumpers showed on the grand prix field and jumped banks, ditches, grobs and water. The hunters jumped rather natural, rustic fences in large rings. But what I liked most was the opportunity to warm up over fences on a real outside course, something some of my riders had never done—or seen—before. Jumping solid, natural fences over uneven terrain at pace with no related distance is something of a lost art.

Bert de Nemethy (and some of his predecessors) showed us how to school horses over gymnastics, combinations and related distances to prepare for great arenas at Aachen (Germany), Hickstead (England) and Rome. He didn't mean for these gymnastics to be an end in themselves.

I remember when I began to apply Bert's schooling sessions to training hunters and equitation riders in the early '60s. Stride counting, bending and flying changes were rather new then. People just galloped and jumped. The emphasis was on pace, not balance and distance. The only stride counting was in the in-and-outs! Now I feel I've helped create a monster.

We have become a nation of mechanized and intellectual riders, not instinctive riders. And when a rider's instinct isn't allowed to develop, a certain weakness and stiffness sets in. Fads, mannerisms and extremes get out of perspective. We had better, stronger and more natural hunter and equitation riders years ago.

We can be as good again. But I must appeal to all horsemen and women in the hunter/jumper world to get the ponies, juniors, amateurs and professionals out of the ring, at least part of the time. We must see a partial return to the true outside course, which should include some uneven terrain, solid-looking fences and unrelated distances.

Only by doing this can we expect to develop in our horses and riders the qualities necessary for good jumping equitation. Instinctive riding includes a sense of pace, line, distance, impulsion and balance. Instinctive riding develops both boldness and caution.

Yes, these things can be taught to some degree in a lesson, but to really learn them you must get the feel in real practice outside the ring.

Show managers, you will say there's no time or place for outside courses. Make a time and a place. And consider doing more for the sport than just running a horse show as a business.

Teachers and trainers, you will say it's too hard for your students to exist outside the protective cocoon of the ring. Present them with the excitement of a challenge. Most of them will learn to love it. Don't worry so much about your pocketbook. You won't starve.

Riders, it's your duty to ask for something better than the standard fare. It's your right to really be allowed to learn to ride. Stand up and speak out.

Our hunter and equitation world has become one repetitive, rather boring gymnastic exercise. This is what's wrong with the hunter division. It's no longer theatrical or exciting. Everyone wears the same clothes, goes at the same (slow) pace, and jumps in the same number of strides. It's even boring for the exhibitors.

Even at Devon (Pa.), which has historically been a good show, the pace has slowed to a crawl. The lines in the hunter classes were chokingly tight and in some classes the fences were jammed into two-thirds of the ring. It's not necessarily the course designers' fault. This practice is the norm and is encouraged by show managers, judges and even professional riders.

Let's stand back and look at the big picture. What's good for the sport isn't always where our next dollar is coming from. I'm a working professional too, and one thing I know is that if the sport is healthy—meaning the values are being upheld—we'll all make a good living for years to come.

I do feel some changes are in the wind. Many people realize that our horsemanship is in trouble. I strongly believe that a great tonic for the ailing is to get outside and start exercising. In horse lingo, this means, "Don't be ring-bound."

It would do my heart good to see us get back, at least part of the time, to the real outside courses of old. You'll all see a difference.

29

Preparing For A Class

August 6, 1993

Any horse show, or any class at a horse show, is just a test. Whether it's the Olympics, ASPCA Maclay Finals, or a pre-green hunter class, it's still just a test of your own and your horse's ability and progress.

You're there to find out how you stack up against the other competitors at your level. What's the quality of your work? And, most importantly, what do you have to work on?

Homework is preparation and showing is execution. This makes me wonder why there's so much teaching at shows today? I wouldn't say it's right, but there's little choice. People and horses are on the road so much today that when they're home all they can do is freshen up. Doing nothing with a horse is a lost art. Nonetheless, the best teaching, training and learning takes place at home. It's called slow work, and that's the only work that really sinks in.

When I get to a show, my first priority is to have a horse in condition, legged-up and looking good. He must be sound.

I abhor having a horse who's sore and uncomfortable. Many, many jumping problems—for both horse and rider—come from a sore horse.

A little phenylbutazone or Banamine never hurt a horse. I believe in a limited amount of medication at a horse show, as a preventative measure. I've shown horses on normal amounts of these medications for years and have never had any problems. Many of these horses are now retired, in good health, and are in their 20s or even 30s. I disagree most adamantly with the new Federation Equestrian International rule that will eliminate all phenylbutazone in Jan. 1. It will drive trainers and riders toward exotic drugs that are bad for horses.

My next priority is rideability. Again, the basis for this lies at home. I pride myself on my own and my students' flatwork. I've always been fascinated by flatwork and I was fortunate in having teachers who were masters in dressage. It must become a way of thinking. Good flatwork provides the relaxation for the horse as well as the rider. Without control, one relies on luck!

I prefer riding a horse "down" rather than longeing. But I will longe hot or extra-fresh horses occasionally. I longe hunters much more than jumpers. I don't like to longe jumpers very often. It's not the best for their legs, especially on hard summer ground.

When I get a horse and rider to their first crossrail before a class, I expect the pair to be beautifully turned out, the horse sound and in peak condition, and both in relaxed control. I don't always jump crossrails, but they never hurt. It's usually a good idea to start over a few low fences since not much good will come without confidence. With crossrails, I concentrate on basic position of the rider and control of the horse, at both trot and canter.

I usually start my schools over very low square oxers instead of crossrails. I rarely, if ever, start over verticals. Oxers open the horse and riders up, get everything going forward and develop scope and confidence. I'll finish over verticals or a narrow oxer. This does just the opposite. It tightens the horse up and emphasizes the horse's form. It's the same principle in dressage—extension before collection.

"The best teaching and training takes place at home."

As a rule, I like going to the ring, be it hunter or jumper, off a slight rub at the verticals. But some horses are so careful they don't need even a gentle rub.

I like ground lines, both true and false. But I will school with no ground lines. It depends on the style and confidence of the horse. I always give generous ground lines at verticals for horses who hang a bit to give them a "knee-jerker." But I don't particularly like wide ground lines at oxers. They're the same as jumping triple bars.

"Older horsemen tend to jump fewer fences than younger horsemen."

As a general rule, it's best to finish your warm-up one or two horses before your turn. That way the horse has time to catch his breath and horse and rider have time to get cleaned up. It's show time, so spit and polish are a *must*.

Just before entering the ring, riders should review the whole course in their minds or even out loud with their trainers. This mental picture, repeated over and over again, will hold the performance together under the pressure of competing. We all suffer from some kind of fear.

158

It's nothing to be ashamed of. It's just important to know how to deal with it. Stage fright always worked *for* me, but it works against some.

Most people warm up horses very well today, although my big criticism is still over-jumping—too many fences, too high and too wide. Older horsemen tend to jump fewer fences than younger horsemen. They've learned the hard way, by breaking horses down.

But the ring tells the tale, either by success or failure. Horses don't lie. And the longevity of a horse who performs well is a tribute to the good horseman warming him up. 🐎

30

Advice For The Prospective Professional Horseman

January 7, 1994

I feel that being a horseman is a privilege, and being a professional horseman is a rare privilege indeed.

The horse may be our most noble creature. He is certainly our most beautiful creature. To be able to work with and make a living with him is something few people are lucky enough to experience. Most of us get so wrapped up in the technical and competitive aspects of equestrian sports that we tend to forget the horse is also a living, feeling being.

I scratch my head in amazement. Young people today leave the junior division, perhaps having won the AHSA Medal or ASPCA Maclay finals, and six months later they are professional horsemen, often out on their own! The apprentice system is over.

I didn't hang out my shingle until I was 26 years old—and I had won both equitation finals, ridden with Bert de Nemethy for four years, ridden the winner of the Grand Prix of Aachen

(West Germany), was a Pan Am gold medalist, Olympic silver medalist, graduated from college, and spent a year studying dressage with Jessica Ransehousen and Gunnar Anderson. But I was still such a green professional horseman that I had to call my friend next door, Bob Freels, every day for advice.

"Actions speak louder than words. It's what you produce that tells the tale."

Professionals in any field are telling the public that they're experts and they can now be paid for their expertise. They are responsible, grown men and women who know how to conduct a business, pay their bills, maintain a riding facility, select and maintain horses properly, teach horsemanship, give riding lessons, train horses, and, in our world, handle people and horses at horse shows.

Because the horse is the reason for being for the professional horseman, every decision and choice must be made in the interest of the horse. To me, the first obligation is the facility where the horses live, the riders ride, and the training takes place. A professional must learn how to physically house horses and riders. This doesn't mean fancy and costly, but it does mean neat, clean, simple and safe.

"Quality work will bring you 10 times more work than poor work."

The next obligation as a professional is the selection, care and handling of horses. The average professional of old was probably better at selecting and caring for horses. He lived with horses daily and was more knowledgeable about conformation, soundness, way of moving, and vices. Today's horsemen are light years ahead of the old school in riding and schooling a horse, but they don't know as much about the horse.

Buying horses is much too risky and expensive to do without an extensive knowledge of the horse, his beauties and defects. We all make mistakes in buying horses. I tell people I'm pretty good at buying horses because I'm 70 percent right! Nobody is 100 percent on the mark when it comes to buying horses.

It's easy to buy a horse (or anything); it's much harder to maintain it. Taking care of a horse beautifully comes well before good training or good riding. A professional must acquire the reputation for being a good, preferably top, caretaker.

Each of us gets along differently with people. I have a rather militant personality in dealing with people I hire in the horse world, probably because all of my teachers were ex-Army officers. This approach won't work for everyone. The people we have to associate with include staff (grooms, managers, secretaries, carpenters, riders, trainers, owners, veterinarians and blacksmiths). It's hard to keep them all in line and content, with themselves and with one another.

Here are some of my beliefs about what a professional horseman should be:

- Be a "neat-nik" with yourself and everything around you. Most people are slobs!
- Never be inhumane to an animal. Yes, be a strong, disciplined, demanding trainer with a horse if necessary, but never inhumane.
- Treat all staff with respect. They will respect you if you work as hard or harder than they. Familiarity breeds contempt.

162

- The professional trainer/teacher is the chief. His or her word goes. It's too dangerous a sport to have more than one person calling the shots. Once a rider, owner, sponsor or groom starts calling the shots, it's all over. Either correct it or send them down the road. If you don't, they'll go down the road anyway.
- Curtail gossip and backstabbing in the barn as much as possible. Get rid of people of people who do this.
- Never compare students or horses. Comparisons are odious. Each has his own good.
- Go out and look for and at horses; it improves your eye.
- Always be on time. It breeds respect.
- Whatever your task, be it big or small, do it to the best of your ability. Quality work will bring you 10 times more work than poor work.
- Never run, or drive fast, around horses. Motorized vehicles and the noise they make have little place around stables. Riding, teaching and training should be quiet and concentrated. Teachers must be able to "watch" their pupils, and riders must be able to "listen" to their horses.
- Alcohol, drugs and smoking have no place around horses. The older I get, the more destructive I see these things are.
- Riding is an athletic endeavor. Stay thin! Inspire people to be athletes.
- The only thing sleazier than blatantly romancing and stealing a customer is doing the same thing to a groom.
- Helping a rider, owner or staff achieve a better opportunity is good, though. This can be done through advertising,

word of mouth, or excellence of service.

- Remember that professionals must live with other professionals for a very, very long time. A professional network, with professional ethics, has stood the test of time. Don't violate this. Don't burn bridges. It will come back to haunt you.
- Do to others—horses, staff, students, clients, veterinarians, trades people, judges, administrators—as you would want them to do to you.
- Young people in the business should watch, listen, and learn. They shouldn't voice their opinions too much, too loudly, or too soon. Actions speak louder than words. It's what you produce that tells the tale.
- Don't unfairly criticize other people's horses.
- Charge correctly for your services so you can pay your bills.
- Never forget or lose respect for the people who helped give you a "leg up" in the horse business, especially parents, other professionals, teachers and owners. Appreciation and respect are great virtues.
- We've all made mistakes in these and other areas. Mistakes are fine if we're willing to learn from them. There has never been such a thing as too good a professional horseman. I'm just honored that it was my lot in life to be one at all.

31

What's Classical And What's Tacky In Turning Out Hunters And Jumpers

March 22, 1996

A few weeks ago, a well-known hunter/jumper exhibitor gave me a long list of her pet peeves regarding turn-out of a horse and rider. I read down this list and thought I should elaborate on it somewhat to pass along to the *Chronicle's* readers. She couldn't be more accurate.

There is usually only one right way when it comes to presenting the horse and rider. And that right way revolves around safety, cleanliness and taste. Nothing should distract the eye from the horse and his workmanlike rider.

• Nylon bridles and girths are no good, for no other reason than they look tacky and cheap. I like high-quality, flat, not-too-wide, not-too-thin, dark brown tack of a most conventional nature. I don't like an excess of fancy stitching. I insist on checking tack for repair and keeping all tack (and everything else) scrupulously clean.

- Colored or argyle polo wraps and bell boots are gaudy and cheap-looking and shouldn't be used. A white, dark brown, or black wrap is acceptable. It's the same for bell boots, although years ago we used a dark red bell boot that didn't look too bad. But I haven't seen them lately.
- Bright colors in any manner should not be used with hunters or jumpers. It distracts from the horse and looks cheap.
- Flashy colors do not dress up horse or rider. They detract.
- Unpolished boots or paddock boots are the worst. I don't allow it. The first rule of good horsemanship is to be clean.

Every night after riding I take off my spurs and boots and clean them—not the next morning. The sweat and dirt have by then started or continued to ruin the leather and stitching.

I have a system for cleaning my spurs and boots: First, I take the spur straps off the spurs to clean everything thoroughly. Then I use a dry rag to get rid of all external dust, dirt and mud. Next I use a wet rag for the sweat and dirt that remains. After the leather is clean, I apply a thin coat of polish and brush until shiny. These stainless steel spurs just need a little warm water and dry cloth. We used to have to use metal polish.

166

I never use conditioners or creams on my boots because it diminishes the shine. Nothing touches my boots but water, polish and myself.

As an exercise in self-discipline, I always do my boots myself.

- Strange-colored breeches in the hunter/jumper world are not OK. Nor are red, green or blue paddock boots. Old traditional values, habits and customs still will always be the best. Gaudy colors only spell cheap and ignorant and distract from the horse. My steel-gray breeches are avant-garde enough, and I certainly wouldn't go farther. Beige, canary, rust and white for certain events are the best colors.
- Horses that walk to the ring with hoof packing and manure still in their feet are a sign of sloppy grooming. This reflects poorly on the rider and the trainer. The rider should be responsible for everything. Riders who have been trained properly should know how to do everything.
- Rainbow reins are about as tacky as anything that's come along in a long time. One does not learn correct rein length by colors, but by good training and habit. I never put knots in the middle of the rein to assist green riders. Riders must learn to control the length of the reins themselves.
- Dirty, grass-stained bits and stirrup irons are another disgrace. Anything like this is an insult to the horse, horsemanship, and the sport. We show respect for our horse by the way we turn out the horse and rider. I simply

could not take a horse out of my barn at a home, let alone at a show, improperly turned out.

- Large, square saddle pads or colored saddle pads don't look good. A saddle pad should contour closely to the saddle and not stick out like a sore thumb. They should be unobtrusive in size and color. I don't mind a perfectly white, smallish baby pad that's square underneath the sheepskin pad. This absorbs the sweat and is nicer for the horse. It also looks good.

- Large, dirty stains on breeches are an instant giveaway that either the saddle is dirty or has not been properly cleaned or has been recently stained. All are wrong. One darkens a saddle through cleaning, use and time, not by staining. Putting stain on saddles ruins breeches. People walking around with dirty breeches are suspect.

- Knee socks higher than a rider's boots also look very, very sloppy. I always wear high, thin, black socks that hold my breeches in place and make it easier to slip on m custom-made Vogel boots. I've always got to remember to fold my socks down at the top so the boot is higher than the sock.

- Pony tails and loose hair drive me crazy—either boys, or girls. Boys with long hair must push every wisp up under their helmets. Of course, I'd prefer boys to get a good, short haircut. Girls up until they're 12 are permitted to wear pigtails on ponies. After that they must use hairnets, push their hair up under their helmets or get a short haircut.

- Neckties flying outside of coats really are unnecessary and look sloppy. If you don't have a tie clip, use a good old-fashioned bandage pin. It's worked for years and we

168

used to consider it very chic.

- Colored yarn should never be braided in to manes. Again, the bright colors distract the eye from the horse. Manes and tails should always be braided with the same color yarn or thread as the color of the hair. Gray horses can be braided in either white or black. The cardinal rule is nothing should be brighter or showier than the horse.
- The more conservative the turn-out, the more elegant it is.
- Manure stains and shavings anywhere outside the stall are just plain dirty. There is really nothing worse nor more insulting to the horse or the sport than to see these unsightly eyesores. Take time to properly clean, bathe and groom your horses in a meticulous way.
- I'm a stickler about body clipping and trimming my horses. It's like a guy getting a haircut. If a horse is going to work hard and has a long coat, he'll get sick. I've always believed that if in doubt about the length of a horse's coat, clip him. It will look better, it's easier to groom, and he'll stay healthier.

Every week, my horses get trimmed with the little clippers. I pay particular attention to the muzzle, face, throatlatch, poll, back of the legs, pasterns, and the coronary band. The poll should be trimmed flat about an inch—the width of a piece of leather—no more.

- There should never be brass on any piece of tack except a brass nameplate on the cantle of the saddle. All of these brass nameplates and tags on bridles, breastplates and martingales are just plain wrong. When they shine, it

169

looks so tacky. Pieces of leather should be marked with a leather stamp on the inside of the leather.

- Some people at horse shows, by their use of a hose and sponge, would be better suited to be firemen. Washing horses is a technique that doesn't include spraying one's neighbors and flooding the stabling area. Courtesy at horse shows is sometimes overlooked.

- Loud trainers (and I admit I've often been one of the worst!) are obnoxious. I've probably inspired generations of these types. Nonetheless, we must "tone it down" from time to time.

- Some exhibitors think it's their right to park anywhere at any time. Parking in the wrong place can be an extreme safety hazard. Horses must be able to pass safely and freely in and out of stabling and schooling areas. Falls, accidents and even fires do happen. Vehicles blocking the wrong passageways are a disaster. Park cars in parking lots.

- Have you ever seen a horse at a dog show? I never bring my dogs to a horse show. But if you do bring them, keep them safely in a stall or on a short rope. Horses can get tangled up in long ropes and leashes tying dogs to tent poles.

- This certainly is one of the most dangerous of my pet peeves: Dogs running in and out of rings are absolutely inexcusable.

- "Holding" the schooling fence eight or 10 horses before one's turn in the ring is selfish and thoughtless. This annoying and most regular occurrence gives no consideration to the exhibitor who goes earlier in the order. Jumping five or six horses out gives one plenty of time to school and then walk around before entering the ring.

- Courtesy and thoughtfulness to others make for the best exhibitors. Nothing beats common sense and a little good taste. 🐎

32

Horsemanship Is For The Horse

June 5, 1998

Everything we do with horses, every rule we follow, is ultimately for the good of the horse. Mucking out a stall, picking out the feet, body clipping, keeping our heels down, doing a shoulder-in, trotting a crossrail, or jumping a bending line should all be for the horse.

Good riding and good training are *not* for the rider's or trainer's ego, they're for the horse.

During junior weekend at the Devon Horse Show & Country Fair (Pa.), all the talk was about how some trainers have been overworking their equitation horses. Well, this isn't new. There have always been drillers. In fact, Otto Heuckeroth, Dave Kelly and even my own mother would get after me when I was a kid for drilling my horses. Hopefully, I've outgrown drilling.

Bill Steinkraus taught me a good lesson. He used to say: "If you can't accomplish something with a horse in one hour, get off, put him away, and try again tomorrow." It was one of the best pieces of advice I've ever received, and I've never forgotten it.

Gunnar Andersen, the great Danish dressage master, rode so well and accomplished so much with his horses in a short time that he rarely rode a horse longer than 40 minutes. As in all good horsemanship, maximum effect with minimum effort.

We Americans have a problem. It's called perfectionism. I am guilty of it. Many of us are guilty of it. It's a good and bad trait. Perfectionism is hard to live with.

The equitation division, which received the brunt of the criticism at Devon for the way trainers overprepared their horses, has become dressage over fences and an end in itself. Good form to produce good function is healthy; good form as an end in itself isn't so healthy.

The Germans have always said that the Americans "die in their beauty." It used to offend me, but now I know what they mean and think they're often right. Equitation today is often studied, mannered, stiff and artificial. It's looking inward at the rider, not outward toward the horse. Equitation is supposed to promote horsemanship and help develop horsemen and horsewomen—not teach young people how to overwork, sour and cripple horses.

Watch how equitation horses move and jump. They are often not very sound. Watch their expressions. They are often lifeless, depressed and bored.

Katie Monahan Prudent was the greatest equitation rider of all time. No, she didn't have the perfect build for the sport. But, along with her enormous talent, she possessed showmanship, poise, invisible aids, a workmanlike yet elegant style, and the go-for-broke attitude of a winner. You always felt she was showing off herself and her horse.

There are also plenty of drillers around the hunter world. Again, the reason is our obsessive-compulsive behavior in the

173

quest for a perfect hunter performance. I was brought up to believe that the show hunter was supposed to simulate horses found in the hunting field and that the fences and courses should do the same.

I've ridden or driven in and around most hunting countries in the world and have yet to see fences that look at all like the fences we ask our hunters to jump. These courses are artificial, soft and far from the truth. When you take the blood and guts out of our sport, you lose a lot. If we would get back to jumping some real fences, that would help.

A hunter performance isn't a dressage test with fences in the way. It's gallop and jump. Or it should be gallop and jump.

What is a hunter? A hunter is an attractive, smooth, Thoroughbred-type horse. He looks through the bridle with class, has a good disposition, and moves low to the ground. He's apparently a good mount to hounds.

I'll always lean toward Thoroughbred-type horses. They can go the distance that often half-breds can't. I like expression and enthusiasm with any horse—not a jaded, stale, dulled horse. A hunter needs to have presence, self-carriage and a pleasing appearance.

The most important characteristic of a good hunter, however, is the quality of his jump. Jumping fences on a good jumper is fun; jumping fences with a bad horse is downright dangerous.

A good jumper is tight and square with his front legs, first and foremost. He follows through and uses himself behind. And, what's most important, he uses his back. He has a round bascule. He's not flat or inverted and doesn't reach, hang or unload with his front legs—nor does he twist in front or behind.

When judging hunters, the following needs to be considered: Hunters should *not* be overflexed. Too little flexion is preferable over too much flexion. Horses should be in a natural frame to gallop across country. Light rubs should be taken into account, but they are only tie-breakers. The same is true for a lead change that's a little late.

Judges need to compare the horses and overall rounds, not just the faults. Judging a class is a constant re-evaluation. Again, we all get bogged down in perfection and quickly lose sight of the forest for the trees.

In hack classes, head wagging (sawing hands) and what's called false flexion (broken necks) should be severely penalized. It's an awful sight to see. The rider's hands and legs should be perfectly still. What has happened to invisible aids? The great art of riding is to produce maximum result with minimum effort.

I like to see horses walk in hack classes. The walk should be ground-covering and full of impulsion. Any tension in the horse is quickly spotted at the walk. Laziness too.

The trot should be long, low and sweeping. "Daisy cutters" are often too flat and stiff. High knee action, padding or winging are penalized. Horses must move well behind, not just in front. Often judges tend to forget to look behind the saddle. Horses should neither drag their hocks nor exhibit too much hock action.

I'm an old-fashioned horseman and a stickler for turn-out. Horses and riders must be well presented in the traditional fashion.

A beautifully groomed horse in good weight, well-trimmed with a braided mane (and sometimes tail) is a must. *Pads of any kind do not belong in the hunter ring!* Remember, you're at a horse show and are presenting your horse. You're not at a circus.

Hunter riders must realize that hunters are ridden in a looser, more extended frame than are jumpers. Nor should the rider's position over fences detract from the performance of the horse. Swinging, kicking lower legs, pivoting on the knees, roached backs, jumping ahead, dropping back, throwing or lifting hands all detract from the overall picture.

Standing up in a pseudo-galloping position at a canter or posting to the canter is not the correct way to canter a horse. The horse must accept the rider's seat.

When it's all said and done, the horse that I generally pin is the horse I'd like to ride. And unless an exhibitor has watched every horse from the same position as the judge, the judge should not be second-guessed. Even then, don't be quick to criticize. Each person has his or her own opinion.

American riders in international circles are known for their attention to detail and obsessive-compulsive behavior toward obtaining perfection. Believe me, jumper riders are not immune to the same malady that affects our hunter and equitation devotees. Practice, practice, practice doesn't make perfect. It makes jumpers sore, stale and bored and teaches them to hit fences. Frank Chapot and I are the co-chefs d'equipe for our USET show jumping team and nothing drives us crazier than to watch some of our riders over-jump.

Gordon Wright used to call it "jump happy." He'd tell us no good would come of it, and he was right. I call these jump-happy types "jumpaholics." Usually, it's a form of insecurity on the rider's part that causes him to jump and jump and jump. A horse has only so many jumps in him. Remember that.

And, remember when you get to a show, your horse either knows his job or doesn't. If he knows his job, keep him fresh and interested. If he doesn't know it by then, it's too late, and he'll learn something by just going in the ring.

33

I've Been Decades Finding That Elusive "Distance"

April 14, 2000

Probably the most elusive element in jumping horses is how to find a distance. This is the question I'm asked most often as an instructor. It obsesses people, and well it might.

Of all the factors in jumping a fence—pace, line, distance, balance and impulsion—distance is probably the most crucial.

Most anybody can learn to establish different speeds and different lines to address specific problems. But the sense of balance and the sense of impulsion as a base—that, of course, is more difficult to acquire.

Still, nothing compares in difficulty to finding a distance. Some people are born with it (Rodney Jenkins, Katie Monahan Prudent and Conrad Homfeld); some people develop it, myself included; and some simply never get it.

The winter of 1947-'48 was the first time I ever jumped a fence. It was at the Ox Ridge Hunt Club in Darien, Conn. Miss Felicia Townsend, the riding mistress at the club, announced I was ready. The fence was literally 2 feet off the ground, a straight rail. (Cross rails were non-existent in those days.)

My mount Peanuts was one of the best school horses ever. She was an attractive bay mare about 14.3 hands, an ex-polo pony. She was smart, safe, smooth and quiet and a good jumper over low fences. In fact, later that spring, I rode in my very first class over fences on her.

Miss "T" put me into my forward jumping position at the end of the ring, told me to reach with my hands, and sent me down over this fence. I was hooked. There was no talk of any distance.

The next few years are foggy in my mind at best, and I'm sure I was even foggier at the time jumping fences. We just grabbed mane and went. If we "got in right," great! If we "got in wrong," we just chipped.

One either had timing or didn't. Raymond Burr had timing. So did Bill Steinkraus, Betty Bosley, Adolph Mogavero, Bobby Burke and Cappy Smith. We looked at our idols, these mortals, who possessed something magical called timing.

I had a great teacher in Gordon Wright and a fabulous junior horse named Game Cock. He was chestnut with a dish face and a lot of white. He could win the hack, the junior hunter, and the equitation classes. He was what was called a machine. Still, I had no "eye" for a fence.

Gordon Wright was so frustrated with my poor timing that he pawned me off to a lowly assistant teacher, Gloria Fiore. She gave me exercises, but to no avail, I just couldn't get it.

I do remember one day at Ox Ridge, around the time when a slight glimmer came, and I started to see or feel when I was "right" or "wrong." It was a start down a long road.

During the mid-'50s, riding my jumpers The Gigolo, War Bride and Gordon's Saxon Woods, my timing felt better. It was probably because I could do something, be more active. Actually, I always felt better riding jumpers than hunters. It was at this time that I figured out if I let a horse go out of the turn, I arrived right much of the time. Again, the leave-your-horse-alone theory.

As I became more prominent riding jumpers, people would ask me to ride their top hunters in the gentlemen's class and the amateur class. It was my greatest fear because I had no eye on a hunter.

I especially remember one year at the National (N.Y.) riding for Miss Eleo Sears, a daunting woman to say the least. Joanie Walsh Hogan put me on at the in-gate and said, "Don't touch them!" Then she turned me loose. I didn't dare touch them, and they won. The Nations Cup and the grand prix looked easy after that class.

At about this same time, Dave Kelley, one of our country's top hunter/jumper professionals of all time, was at the top of his game. He held a theory that if he had eight good fences, even without a lot of pace, he would win some kind of ribbon and by accumulating ribbons he would become champion. Dave, a jumper rider also, was considered a "hand-rider" at that time. Cappy Smith worked under the same principle. And so around 1960 the "leave-alone" school was about to fade out and subtle forms of hand riding were about to come in.

It was about this time at Madison Square Garden that Peggy Augustus Lavery and her husband, Tom, had a beautiful Argentine Thoroughbred named Sutton Place. He was hot horse and a gray. He jumped quite well and always won the model.

Tommy was trying to teach her to keep a horse in hand and place him at his fences. She stated that she hated this way of riding, couldn't and wouldn't do it, and for all intents and purposes, hung up her tack. Slower, more precise riding was about to come into its own and with it the emphasis on "eye," striding and distance.

Bert de Nemethy came onto the scene at the U.S. Equestrian Team in 1955. By the early 1960s, he was the guru, not only of our country, but also of the world. His horses and riders went in a measured, controlled, smooth way. Bert's whole system of training revolved around distance and balance. He taught horses these two factors through cavaletti and gymnastics. Because of Bert's tape measure, we saw and learned every possible distance. However, Bert did not talk much about seeing a distance from the canter—that was to come later.

"Probably the most elusive element in jumping horses is how to find a distance."

I came fresh off the team into the professional ranks in 1964 and, of course, had to deal with hunters and equitation horses, as well as jumpers. All of my recent training with Bert had revolved around numbers of strides between fences. This, of course, was unheard of in the day with hunters. One either came "right" to a fence or "wrong." There was no line with a number attached to it. It was the Dark Ages.

"Nothing beats a natural eye for a fence. But it's not yet in a pill."

It was early in the spring, and we were at the Ox Ridge junior indoor show. I had a great riding girl at the time name Jen Marsden. She had a good-jumping but bad-moving chestnut mare that she used as a junior hunter and an equitation horse. I figured if striding had worked on jumpers, why wouldn't it work on hunters?

181

Using this system, Jen beat many better horses that weekend. Her consistency came from not only having a brilliant natural eye for a fence, but her ability to know the exact number of strides between fences, like everybody does today.

As a professional in the mid-'60s, I could ride a jumper and see my fences quite well. On a hunter, I was nothing short of a disaster. I had not yet learned the technique of reliably finding a "spot," either as a rider or as a teacher.

Benny O'Meara was at the pinnacle of his career at this time. He died in the spring of 1966. Benny, just by his presence, taught us all so much about jumping, schooling and showing horses. He helped make stars out of people such as Kathy Kusner, Rodney Jenkins and Carl Knee. Benny got Kathy out of a rather stiff mold and gave her technique.

Benny had a theory that if you came out of the turn easing off the horse's mouth, it put the rider in a neutral (and, I must say enviable) position where he could either take back and shorten into the distance or let go still more and lengthen into the distance.

By the late 1960s, striding between fences set closely together was more of the norm. Of course, there were still big outside courses where one still had to gallop and jump and eyeball the fences, which were set very far apart. Nonetheless, people were starting to talk distance and how to see a spot.

I remember conducting a teacher's clinic out at the Old Mill Farm on Long Island. It was during the last session after three long, grueling days. Two nice ladies from North Carolina were very frustrated because they couldn't teach a pony rider to see a spot as well as this other child in North Carolina who won all the classes. I suggested several exercises and gave some lengthy demonstrations. It was only after all this that I found out the other child was none other than Jane Womble, one of the great women riders this country was to produce. These teachers were beating their heads against a stone wall trying to beat Jane.

The precision, accuracy and timing that we see today, as well as the complete understanding of finding a distance, probably crystallized into a system during the 1970s. By that time the "leave 'em alone," run–and–jump school had pretty much vanished. Rodney Jenkins, Bernie Traurig and Katie Prudent not only had fantastic natural eyes, but they also had control over them and could do with them what they wanted. They could ride hunters and jumpers with equal splendor.

From the 1970s to the present, the subject of distance has been uppermost in riders', teachers' and trainers' minds. Yes, there are valuable exercises that can improve one's sense of timing. To understand "looking" versus "seeing" is important. So is the ability to jump at different rates of speed. Jumping every possible line, distance problem and combination can only enhance a feel for distance.

Soft arms, and going with the horse off a turn, enable one to better see a distance. Understanding the *long* first option as well as the *short* second option is most important.

Nothing beats a natural eye for a fence. But for those of us who weren't born so lucky, there's hope. All it takes is intelligence, understanding, work and practice. It's not yet in a pill. 🐎

34

The Releases I Teach

November 10, 2000

Since I'm more of an educated horseman than a natural horseman, I've always been fascinated by the technical details of the sport. Whether it regarded the horse's conformation, way of going, style of jumping or the rider's position, use of aids, or correct dressage, I've always wanted to understand the mechanics of how and why. This has beckoned me as a lifelong quest.

And so it is with hands. Teaching and developing legs on a rider is relatively easy and takes a relatively short time. Developing a seat is much harder and takes much longer, usually about 10 years. (Most of the time without stirrups, if one really wants to have a seat!)

But to develop "educated" hands takes a lifetime at best. To be perfectly honest, most people never acquire educated hands. They don't have the feel, the patience or the time.

The great principle of riding is called the "give and take," but, in truth, we should say "take and give." There is a big difference, and that's the way it really works.

One applies pressure, then releases it, not the other way around. The "take" on a horse's mouth is when any pressure is applied to do anything: slowing, stopping, bending, turning or balancing the horse. The "give" is simply the cessation of pressure when the horse responds, or even before the horse responds.

Just as in life, it is much more difficult for people to give than to take. It is also a self-preservation, defensive reaction for most people to grab a horse's mouth when they feel at all insecure, which is most of the time.

The single most important attribute of the "give" is that it promotes and enables self-carriage, the *sine qua non* of a light horse. There is very little self-carriage today due to the prevalent misinterpretation of the German school of riding.

Our own incomparable Rodney Jenkins demonstrated self-carriage every time he rode a horse, as did Kathy Kusner and Ben O'Meara. Actually, to contradict myself a little bit, most of the truly top riders of the world, both in dressage and jumping do understand and appreciate self-carriage.

Gordon Wright isolated, formalized and taught the long release 50 years ago, in his bible, *Learning to Ride, Hunt, and Show*. He demanded that the rider's hands move halfway up the crest of the neck and press down during elementary jumping. If the rider's hands pulled back during flight, instead of pushing down, he insisted on grabbing mane. I don't remember neck straps back then because all horses had manes.

The long release has distinct advantages for beginners. It ensures complete freedom for the horse, allowing him to gesture with his balancing agent, his head and neck. And by moving the hands forward halfway up the crest of the neck, it puts the rider's upper body into a correct jumping position—forward. This is certainly the correct jumping position for elementary riders.

The long release caught on with advanced riders too. In fact, it caught on too much! It's a very useful technique when schooling green horses to get them to think for themselves. Hunters are presented well to a judge with a long release. It shows a "loose horse." And this release works very well when purposely dropping a horse in order to get a rub and wake him up.

Gordon Wright's pupils would graduate from the elementary long release to jumping out of hand on the automatic release. Of course, many of his students were never allowed to practice the automatic release. They were not good enough, nor would they ever be.

Gordon introduced the short release later in his career. Being the genius he was, he realized he needed something between the two releases that he already taught.

When a rider uses a short release, his hands only move and inch or two up the horse's crest. They rest and press down, just as in the long release. The advantage of the short release is, of course, control, but it doesn't necessarily put the rider forward in to the jumping position. That's why the short release should never be introduced before an intermediate level of jumping.

Assuming a jumping position must be automatic for a rider before attempting a short release. This release still gives the horse freedom of his head and neck and yet allows his rider much more control. Riders can use the short release in hunter, jumper and equitation classes, as long as they're at least intermediate level riders.

Gordon taught me later in his life not to teach an automatic release (jumping out of hand) from a long release, but always from a short release. And it makes perfect sense. It's more progressive.

The automatic release is rarely seen today. It's on the endangered species list. It's all but extinct. People don't know how to teach it or use it like they did in the 1950s and 1960s. All of Bert de Nemethy's, Gordon Wright's and Jimmy Williams' advanced students jumped "out of hand." It was commonplace and done well.

"The automatic release is rarely seen today."

What is the automatic release all about? It's about consistency, the maintenance of a straight line, elbow to mouth, as well as soft contact throughout the jump. By this time in a rider's career, he doesn't need the neck of the horse to support his upper body. Earlier on, he does need to put the weight of his upper body into his hands, but not now.

In fact, when correctly executing the automatic release, a rider doesn't touch the neck of the horse. The ability to do this requires complete security in the saddle, balance and timing.

"The long release has distinct advantages for beginners."

What is a rotation? A rotation is when the hands rotate back and up off the horse's neck and pull the horse's mouth. Done by a beginner or a "butcher," a rotation is the cardinal sin. They hit the horse in the mouth. When done by an advanced jumping artist, a rotation is an invaluable technique, however. Bill Steinkraus did it and advocated it all the time.

A rotation is when one "nips" or lifts the horse off the ground. I don't like it. It gets the horse dependent on the rider's hands, the opposite of self-carriage. I will use it, however, to

187

save my neck from a fall or save a rail in a jumper class, especially going at speed.

To use a rotation on a hunter, the horse must be extremely obedient. Some judges won't pin a horse if the rider helps him up off the ground, and I'm one of them! While this technique has no place in the hunter ring, it is useful to learn when riding jumpers.

Essentially, this is an overview of how to use your hands when jumping horses. Any other hands you see are only variations of these techniques, these techniques done wrong, or bad habits.

It's most important for all riders to master the technique that is appropriate for their level before moving on. At all costs, avoid the mistakes that so many do—to try something you're not ready for.

Remember, hands take a long, long time to acquire, so be patient.

35

Observations I've Made While Teaching

January 11, 2002

I've been teaching extensively the past three months, it seems more than ever, and there are some points I've noticed that need clarification. Unless teachers review the classics of riding and jumping literature on a regular basis, they will become stale and fall prey to fashions and fads. For me the great supplement to knowledge is reading books.

STIRRUP POSITION: No only for aesthetics, but also for ankle flexibility and in order to better keep the heels down, the stirrup iron belongs on the ball of the foot, the stirrup diagonally on the foot (outside branch leading), and the little toes touching the outside branch. It's preferable to have a heavy-duty iron (no hinged stirrups) with stirrup pads that grip.

STIRRUP LENGTH: The better the rider, the more range he must have in length of stirrup according to what he is doing. Elementary riders should stick to an all-purpose length of iron, suitable for riding and jumping. Intermediate riders should have a slight differentiation, say a hole longer for flat work than for jumping. Advanced riders could have a spread of from two to four holes, depending on the height of the fences they're jumping. Most people are lazy about this and, as a consequence, develop a "chair" seat.

HEELS DOWN: To keep one's heels down is of the utmost importance in riding and jumping. It provides us with all-important security in the saddle and with an independent and, if need be, a strong leg grip. Slack calf muscles are useless on a horse. In order to learn to keep the heels down, it's good for every rider to spend some of the time in suspension or standing in the stirrups (two-point contact). It's simply the correct distribution of weight. If people ride too long in their irons and never get out of the saddle, they will never get their heels down.

BASE OF SUPPORT: The crotch and seat bones belong near the front of the saddle for slow work with longer stirrups. Not only is the horse's back stronger than his loins, but this also enables the rider to follow the horse's movement through the seat and lower back. Of course for fast work with shorter stirrups, the buttocks shift more toward the back of the saddle.

UPPER BODY: The upper body at the standstill and for backing is imperceptibly in front of the vertical, ready to be with the horse when he moves off. At the sitting trot and the canter only about 5 degrees in front of the vertical; for posting the trot, galloping, and jumping about 30 degrees in front of the vertical. That is our basic, median position at the different gaits. Of course, for special needs we can shift to the front or but move over to the rear (behind the motion).

HANDS: Most of the time we should ride with a straight line from the elbow to the horse's mouth. That is to say with a "star-gazer" (high-headed horse) we ride with higher hands. In showing off a hunter we ride with a broken line below the mouth (low hands) to hide the hands. It's best to ride a "stopper" with a broken line above the mouth so he can't drop his head.

Today many people mistakenly ride with too low a hand and "sawing" hands, vainly trying to lower a horse's head the wrong and painful way. In order to lower a horse's head, it's best to raise the hands, close the hands, and wait for the horse. Easier said than done.

AIDS: The horse must move forward from both legs of the rider. However, the inside leg is dominant, stronger. The horse must come back from both hands, the outside one being dominant or stronger. If practiced in this way, it affects the whole horse better, quicker, stronger.

CORNERS: Start with the outside rein, which should open to the outside, maintaining the track at the speed. The inside rein (indirect rein in front of the withers) displaces the horse's weight from the inside to outside shoulder and also bends the neck of the horse. Do not overbend the neck to the inside. The inside leg not only maintains the impulsion, but also bends the horse, while the outside leg goes back about a hand to guard the hindquarters.

It's also good to practice corners and turns using the opening, bearing and pulling reins. Teach horses and riders to turn using a variety of rein and leg combinations.

RHYTHM: Rhythm always must have regularity first. Then it must be coupled with the right amount of impulsion. Extension and speed do not necessarily mean that a horse has sufficient impulsion. In fact, when teaching the "lesson of the leg" through the whip or the spurs, hold the horse back (half-halt). Impulsion is the horse thinking forward with more animation and higher, more active hind legs.

TRACKING: One must know where a horse's feet are. First,

191

his shoulders and his hindquarters. Through his influences, the rider first must be able to make the horse "track straight"—left hind, left front, right hind, right front. Then he can understand shoulder-in, haunches-in and half-pass. People are usually so fixated on the head and neck that they forget the whole horse.

"We all tend to drift into gimmicks, fashions and fads."

WITH THE MOTION: It's best for any and every rider to master posting and jumping "with the motion" before attempting the much more complete "behind the motion." "Ahead of the motion," of course, is never right, but one doesn't often see that anymore. The advantage to riding "with the motion" is the smoothness and ease for both horse and rider. One is with the horse before he posts; one is with the jump before the jumps. To differentiate, the rider closes his hip angle, inclines to the front about 30 degrees, and is thrown forward and upward (with the motion).

"Our job is to try to maintain a classic line."

Riding "behind the motion," the rider goes upward and forward, catching up with his horse. His hip angle is open and his upper body is on the vertical. Personally, I like teaching both methods to more advanced riders.

TWO-POINT VS. THREE-POINT CONTACT: For galloping on straight lines or gradual turns, two-point contact is used (both legs on the horse). For sharper turns and the approach to a jump, three-point contact is used (both legs and the seat). For galloping and

192

jumping, both positions should be practiced. Riders sit down in the saddle too much today, which is bad for their riding and bad for their horse. Good trainers teach the horse self-balance or self-carriage. Teach the horse to go with less—less hand, less leg, less seat.

EYES: We all look down too much. Check yourself the next time you ride. I know I look down too much. A good exercise is to look at focal points when you ride. The instructor makes an ideal focal point. It's like driving a car. Keep your eyes on the road.

EQUILIBRIUM: (Balance) I'm doing a lot of grid work again. No-stride in-and-outs with no stirrups, no reins, no sticks, no spurs. The fences are very low (about 2'6") and the riders quickly develop security, balance, coordination and confidence. We used to do a lot of this work and then forgot it.

JUMPING OUT OF HAND: If you do a lot of grid work, jumping out of hand (automatic release) for the more advanced rider will be within reach, although it does take practice. This release gives the rider total control. It is a dying art because we are all lazy and depend on the neck of the horse too much for support.

As I've said, these are just some of the points and techniques that I've observed, both here and in other countries, which need to be worked on to improve our riding, teaching and training. We all tend to drift into gimmicks, fashions and fads. Our job is to try to maintain a classic line, no matter what horses we ride and train and no matter whom we teach. Fashions come and go. Style never changes.

36

Bill Steinkraus' Two Dozen Useful Aphorisms

November 7, 2003

Several months ago, my friend Judy Richter kindly sent me a copy of Bill Steinkraus' revised edition of his classic book *Reflections on Riding and Jumping.* Ever since, I've read it, reread it, underlined it, made my marginal notes, and digested it.

I have always loved to read inspirational riding material. It helps my teaching, which, of course, I do a lot of.

Bill Steinkraus wasn't one of my teachers as a young man. But I watched him school Maud Farrell's horses early on at Ox Ridge (Conn.), and I watched him at many horse shows, rode with him from time to time, and of course, later on became his teammate at the U.S. Equestrian Team. So Billy was one of my principal influences, my mentor.

Billy and Trafalgar Square Publishing have very generously allowed me to take some of his written material and elaborate from my own perspective.

I grew up hearing, seeing and using many of Billy's aphorisms, and they always kept me in good stead. And so here are Two Dozen of Bill Steinkraus' Useful Aphorisms. My comments are strictly from my own personal riding experience, not his.

No. 1. Get your tack and equipment just right, and then forget about it and concentrate on the horse.

Bill Steinkraus was the most meticulous man I have ever ridden with when it came to the quality, make, repair, and cleanliness of his own personal attire and equipment and of his tack. Down to his gloves, hat, whip and spurs—it had to be just so.

He was very particular in fitting a bridle to a particular horse and always preferred pelhams. His equipment, his tack, and his horse were all scrupulously clean before he mounted. Everything down to the tiniest detail was in perfect order. Now all he had to do was ride the horse!

No. 2. The horse is bigger than you are, and it should carry you. The quieter you sit, the easier this will be for the horse.

Billy exemplified this principle of self-carriage for the horse. He appeared to do nothing. If you have to use your driving aids a great deal (legs, weight, voice), your horse hasn't been properly trained to them. If you have to use your restraining aids a great deal (hands, weight, voice), your horse hasn't been properly trained to them.

No. 3. The horse's engine is in the rear. Thus, you must ride your horse from behind and not focus on the forehand simply because you can see it.

Go to the next horse show. How many people are hand-riding on the flat? (Most of them.) How many people are riding leg to hand? (Few of them.) How many horses are "connected" and truly on the bit? (Again, few.)

No. 4. It takes two to pull. Don't pull, push.

Once a hot, strong horse accepts your leg and seat, he's no longer hot and strong. Once a cold horse really accepts your leg and is in front of the leg, he's no longer cold. All horses must be taught to accept your driving aids. Then their mouths will improve immeasurably.

No. 5. For your horse to be keen but submissive, it must be calm, straight and forward.

Calm is first. Calm must permeate everything when you work around a horse, or else you cannot proceed. Forwardness is absolutely indispensable. Once cannot go forward, backward, left or right without the horse "thinking" forward. Straightness is the essence of control; it is the very first step of collection. Keep your horse tracking straight.

No. 6. When the horse isn't straight, the hollow side is the difficult side.

You see this a lot at the horse shows today. The horse escapes the aids by overbending to the inside. Remember, whatever you teach a horse, he'll use against you.

No. 7. The inside rein controls the bending; the outside rein controls the speed.

We see too much inside rein today. Let's start with the dominant inside leg, which puts the horse to the dominant outside rein, which is the half-halt rein, which controls the horse. A well-ridden horse is very little on the inside rein.

"Once you've used and aid, put it back."

"The horse's engine is in the rear."

No. 8. Never rest your hands on the horse's mouth. You make a contract with it: you carry your head and I'll carry my hands.

One of my most memorable riding lessons from Billy was how to get a horse's head down. Raise your hands! One's hands can always go higher than the horse's head. He'll seek to escape this pressure by going the other way—down. I see too many low hands, spread hands, and sawing hands. Horses hate this, and they either go above the bit or behind the bit.

No. 9. If the horse can't learn to accept what you are doing, it isn't any good.

Training horses is love (sometimes tough love), not war. When you see someone always fighting with their horses, they don't understand. And neither do the poor horses. Study and practice classic techniques until you understand them and they work for you.

No. 10. Once you've used aid, put it back.

This has to do with active versus passive aids. Once the horse has responded and yielded, relax the pressure. That is the reward.

Then he'll look to respond quicker the next time. Billy's advice is the basis of self-carriage.

No. 11. You can exaggerate every virtue into a defect.

I'm sure Billy was thinking of the "crest release." I know I am. The long crest release is a virtue for beginner riders or when working with very green horses. After that, there are better ways to use your hands when jumping, such as the "short release" and the "automatic release" (the following hand). The crest release is exaggerated and often used grotesquely.

No. 12. Always carry a stick, then you will seldom need it.

This is a truism if I ever hard one. For any serious riding or schooling, you should know how to use it in a variety of ways. Any and every horse can be taught to accept a stick if you carry it every day and don't abuse him with it.

No. 13. If you've given something a fair trial and it still doesn't work, try something else—even the opposite.

We all tend to be set in our ways and narrow-minded when working with horses. Be open-minded and imaginative, and be willing to change.

No. 14. Know when to start and when to stop. Know when to resist and when to reward.

This piece of advice takes lots of experience dealing with lots of different horses. Some people hate to confront an issue head-on with a horse. Some people don't know when to stop. They're drillers and killers. They're the worst.

No. 15. If you're going to have a fight, you pick the time and place.

I'm constantly setting up situations where I know I'll get small resistances so I can break them up. Just a simple thing, like getting a horse through a puddle. Once that is accomplished, the liverpool and the open water won't be such a task.

No. 16. What you can't accomplish in an hour should usually be put off until tomorrow.

This is a great piece of advice I learned from Billy. I rarely ride a horse more than 50 minutes, if that, in training. Put your ego aside and put your horse back in the barn and try again tomorrow. Perhaps try a different tactic.

No. 17. You can think your way out of many problems faster than you can ride your way out of them.

A few examples of this are: Check your tack thoroughly before mounting. Make sure your off stirrup is down before mounting and that your stirrups are approximately your length. Keep your foot in the stirrup when adjusting the irons. Always have a short rein with a feel of your horse's mouth before going to a faster pace. I could go on, and on, and on.

No. 18. When the horse jumps, you go with it, not the other way around.

Excess motion in the hunter/jumper ring is equally, if not more, appalling than in the dressage ring. Invisibility of aids, self-carriage and wait for your horse are all truisms. Learn what those terms mean and practice the principles.

No. 19. Don't let over-jumping or dull routine erode the horse's desire to jump cleanly. It's hard to jump clear rounds if the horse isn't trying.

This is probably the best single piece of advice Billy could give you. Drilling a horse until he is stale and sore is the worst thing you can do. Once a horse has lost his "try," there is nothing you can do except let him freshen up. And that can take weeks, months or never. The cleanest jumper is a fresh horse.

No. 20. Never give up until the rail hits the ground.

One often has to fight to jump clear. All winning jumper riders somehow know how to leave the jumps up, no matter how tight a spot they get in. Watch Margie Engle!

No. 21. Young horses are like children—give them a lot of love, but don't let them get away with anything.

Love, coupled with discipline, is the *sine qua non* of horse training. Disobedience, resistances and evasions tend to grow like weeds.

No. 22. In practice, do things as perfectly as you can; in competition, do what you have to do.

Americans have always been chided by their European counterparts about dying in their beauty. And rightly so. Often our technique and style are better, but they, as a rule, are tougher competitors.

No. 23. Never fight the oats.

Many horses cannot stand prosperity. It is impossible to train a horse who is always "above himself."

No. 24. The harder you work, the luckier you get.

Nowadays, a lot of people talk over dinner about where they hope to get in the horse game—win the ASPCA Maclay Finals, be amateur-owner hunter champion at Devon (Pa.), ride grand prix, or get on the Olympic team. Usually those are the "talkers." It's the "workers" who attain those lofty goals.

Aren't Bill Steinkraus' aphorisms wonderful? They are little gems, pearls of wisdom that keep you on the right track. That's why I had to share them with you.

Now go out and get his book. You can't learn to ride from a book, but it can sure help.

I've Always Been Devoted To The Forward Seat

Tricia Booker photo

37

Whatever Happened To The Forward Seat?

October 3, 1992

Gordon Wright produced so many teachers and trainers who, in turn, produced so many people who ride hunters and jumpers today. The list would run into the thousands—it's too long to even begin.

Vladimir Littauer taught Jane Marshall Dillon (Joe Fargis' teacher), Bernie Traurig and Dr. Walter Kees (Timmy Kees' father), and many more.

Both of these men were guided in spirit, if not in fact, by the principles of Harry D. Chamberlin and his Ft. Riley cohorts (including Co. John B. Wofford). They would be turning over in their graves if they could see what has become of their beloved forward seat.

Gordon Wright always taught me: "There's not enough time to talk about what is right. Concentrate and work on what is wrong." Again his wisdom has proven true. Let's look at what's wrong with the equitation division today, not what's right.

What has happened to good, basic horsemanship? To me, horsemanship begins with love of the horse. This love encompasses beautiful care, conditioning and the turn-out of the animal.

Only a handful of the horses entering the ring at the Northeast Regional Maclay in Port Jervis, N.Y., were presented in tip-top condition. A few were spit and polish. The others were lacking decent weight or show coats, weren't perfectly clean, or lacked great braiding jobs.

And when they started galloping and jumping, a sadder tale was to be told. Many galloped sore, which shortened their strides, lost scope, and caused them to hit lots of fences. I have rarely judged so many knockdowns—and it wasn't the fault of the excellent course designed by manager Bill Glass.

These horses were stale, bored, drilled and overjumped. Something is artificial and wrong about our whole showing system today. And I'm not excluding the hunter and jumper divisions. The biggest tragedy of all is that this system seems not to be conducive to producing top-class horsemen for the future.

Now to the riding. Many people try to gallop and jump (and even do dressage) with too long a stirrup. This has harmful repercussions for the rest of the rider's body. The stirrup iron should hit just at the bottom of the ankle bone. Then the rider will produce angles at the ankle, knee and hip. The knee angle, or lack of it, tells whether a rider is reaching for his stirrups or not. Properly adjusted stirrups not only give the rider sufficient support and security, but they also allow a rider to lean forward and alleviate a horse's back.

This light, forward position rests both the horse and the rider. That's why we post the trot instead of always sitting to it. At the canter, a very collected gallop, riders should sit in the saddle with their upper bodies ever so slightly in front of the vertical. Galloping and jumping is faster, and we must allow the horse to use his back.

The galloping/jumping position is usually, but not always, inclined forward. For straight lines, we stand up a little bit (two-point contact); approaching a fence or turning, we sink down in the saddle (three-point contact). We only need to get behind the motion of the horse (or behind the vertical) for maximum drive or restraint. This shouldn't be the normal position, but rather the exceptional one.

By always telling elementary or intermediate riders to "sit up," teachers produce riders with upper bodies that either "duck" at the fences, jump ahead of the horse, or drop back in the air. These are most serious jumping faults, and we saw a lot of them at the Maclay regionals. Too many young riders are behind their horses instead of in the middle of their horses!

The head and eyes are also a problem. As Mary Mairs Chapot, my co-judge and one of the greatest stylists I've ever seen, said, "Some of the riders need a martingale." Quite a few riders had their heads too high, which is a symptom of posing.

What happened to a straight line from the rider's elbow to the horse's mouth? It's always a simple and safe thing to teach. Most of the

204

Maclay riders used a broken line below the horse's mouth (hands too low) as they tried to get the horse's head down. Over fences, we saw a lot using a broken line above the mouth (hands too high), especially during the flight of the jump.

This "lift" or "rotation" spoils a horse's mouth in the air, causes flat jumping, and looks awful. As the rider releases the horse's mouth, the hands pop up above the crest of the neck. This is not a correct crest release and diametrically opposed to an automatic release, where the hands should follow the horse's mouth down. In judging equitation (and hunters too), more must be evaluated than how the horse and rider meet the fence, the number of strides, cross-cantering, swapping leads, and other more obvious mistakes. Judges must also consider the quality, feel, talent and basic position of the rider more than they do today. Too many judge mechanically, without truly evaluating the horses and riders.

Now let's get constructive. My first suggestion, to myself and to others, is always to read. There are many books as good or better than mine. Look for authors with a grand philosophy and a past-performance record. Wright, Littauer, de Nemethy and Steinkraus are some of the greatest American authors. There are also great European authors.

Go to horse shows and watch the grand prix riders. Watch the famous and successful ones. Watch the ones with style. See which horses are conditioned and turned out well. Watch the mechanics and how the riders' bodies work. Copy these riders. It's often far removed from what we had to judge at Port Jervis.

Trainers, you have to learn to teach what you believe is right. You don't have to teach what other people teach. Go the clinics, watch tapes, stick to your guns, to what you believe. There are too many sheep today. And many are going over the cliff.

All of us have the duty to protect horsemanship in its entirety, not just to make more money. The equitation division has been our national treasure for years and will only remain our secret weapon if we watch and protect it.

38

Style—A Time For Review

November 26, 1993

In the horse business, this time of year is historically a time to pull up, to review, to turn horses out, and to concentrate on slow work with horses and riders. In many cases, Medal/Maclay riders especially, it's the only time of year (there isn't much "slack" time later) to stamp a rider.

I always try to spend some time during the indoor shows back East to study what people are doing and how they are riding. I've ridden, trained, judged or watched every AHSA Medal and ASPCA Maclay final since I first rode at the old Madison Square Garden in 1950. I've seen the styles and trends come and go. By watching these classes, I get food for thought. This helps my teaching during the winter at various clinics around the country and around the world.

The rider's body is divided into four parts. The leg is from the knee on down. The base of support includes the thighs and seat, all parts touching the saddle. The upper body is all parts above the base. And hands and arms make up the fourth part. Balance is all the parts working correctly together.

In teaching, training and riding, it's better to concentrate on and correct one part at a time. That's the quick way to do it. Working generally, rather than specifically, is the slow way.

This year I started my winter clinic season with a three-day teachers' clinic at my farm in New Jersey. I focused mainly on correcting faults, trends and styles that I had seen while judging this year's AHSA Medal Finals and watching the Maclay Finals.

Starting with the leg, a percentage today ride too long; but not as many as a few years ago. This is probably the result of the big—and often good—influence of dressage on hunter seat equitation. You must remember that dressage riders all over the world often ride too long.

Too long a stirrup can be worse than too short a stirrup, especially for galloping and jumping, where support for the rider and freedom for the horse really counts. It's very hard to get the heels down with too long a stirrup. By reaching for the stirrups, the leg is looser and weaker. Make sure that the stirrup iron hits the bottom of the ankle bone.

Other direct results of a too-long stirrup are riders jumping ahead of their horses, ducking or dropping back over fences. This lack of support causes riders to compensate by trying to catch up with their horse. Not being successful, they drop back.

Today, the base of support is often too deep for galloping and jumping. Of course, the long stirrups and tight ring courses promote this position. Many people canter courses today; they don't gallop. It's a different rate of speed.

By shortening the stirrup a bit, riders are able to gallop and jump "up" (two-point contact) and "down" (three-point contact). This is the best, easiest and prettiest way. All "down" is behind the motion—harder for the horse and rider. All "up" is ahead of the motion, which is worse—no control.

One of the biggest problems today, and 80 percent of the equitation riders do it wrong, is the use of the upper body. The upper body changes at the different gaits. While sitting the trot and the canter, it approaches the vertical, but for posting and galloping (hunter seat equitation) it should be inclined forward.

When the upper body is inclined forward, riders come down into the saddle with their crotch (soft). When the upper body is on the vertical, riders hit the saddle with their buttocks (strong). While this second method is right for stoppers, and extraordinary fences, if it is used all the time it encourages the upper body faults mentioned before—ducking (throwing), jumping ahead and dropping back in the air.

Many, many equitation riders today have these faults. The upper body should not do the work for the horse; nor should it hinder the horse.

Too short a rein in equitation is far too common. It's emphasized by teachers in order to please judges who think a too-short rein is correct. Too long a rein is the lesser of two evils. Then, at least, even if control is compromised, the horse can better use his head and neck. Basic position for hands, in flatwork and galloping, is over and slightly in front of the horse's withers.

"Many people canter the courses today; they don't gallop. It's a different sort of speed."

"One of the biggest problems today, and 80 percent of the equitation riders do it wrong, is the use of the upper body."

A funny syndrome with hands has developed over the last few years. People ride with their hands too low (trying in vain to hold or pull the horse's head down!). This is called a broken line below the mouth. Then they release their horses at a jump with hands too high, lifting and/or throwing them over. It's safer to try and maintain a straight line from elbow to mouth on the approach, during the flight, and landing after a fence. Try to get rid of broken lines.

Another common fault with hands today is, as Bill Steinkraus pointed out to me several years back, that they are "hand-cuffed" together. People are not encouraged, nor sometimes allowed, to use the opening or leading rein. This only limits one's control and definitely promotes stiffness.

The picture of hands today in the show ring often leaves a lot to be desired. I'd advise the teachers to do more than ever with the correct use of the long, short and automatic releases.

In correct teaching and learning, there is always something wrong and something could always be better. There is really not the time to talk about what people do right; rather it's more constructive to use lesson time on what's wrong. By sticking to our "classical guns," we'll ride better in the long run, and our horses will jump better. It's up to our teachers, trainers and judges to see that things are done right.

39

The Decline Of Style

November 4, 1994

What disturbed me most as I observed the AHSA Hunter Seat Equitation Medal Finals in Harrisburg, Pa., was the lack of style. Yes, more than 200 riders competed, the course was excellent, and the judging was fair and square. The champion, Keri Potter, and the reserve champion, Ainsley Vance, had very good form. But it really bothered me that most of the rest just didn't have any style.

We must go back to the great hunter/jumper riders and teachers of the '50s. Bill Steinkraus, Raymond Burr, Gordon Wright, Bert de Nemethy, Vladimir Littauer, Jimmy Williams and Jane Marshall Dillon all demonstrated and insisted on style in their work. Style was ridden, taught and judged.

But not so much today. Judges count strictly the execution of the round—the horse's lead, the distance, and the number of strides. These things are all most important, but style comes first because it's even more fundamental.

You can easily ride, judge or teach style by breaking the rider's body down into five parts: The leg (from the knee on down), the base of support (thighs and seat), the upper body (all parts above the base), hands and arms. Balance or equilibrium is when all parts are working correctly together.

Today, a good majority of riders, say 70 percent, have a good leg position. An educated leg means the heels are down and just behind the girth, the ankles flexed, the toes out just a shade, and the calf in contact with the horse. Riders must also have the right length stirrup for hunter or equitation.

The small percentage who don't have good leg position probably ride with too long a stirrup, which destabilizes the leg, raises the heel, and loosens the leg. Two good exercises help the legs—standing in the stirrups (two-point contact) and riding without stirrups.

Next comes the base of support, the thighs and seat. The rider's weight should rest on the crotch and seat (pelvic) bones, not on the flat of the buttocks and the base of the spine. Riders should follow the movement of the horse's back through their seats. Galloping and jumping on the vertical, as is often done today, always produces a bumpy, rough ride. Absorbing the shock through the crotch, instead of the buttocks, is much softer and smoother.

Again, the best exercise—and I mean this only as an exercise—to bring the weight forward into the crotch instead of back into the buttocks is the use of two-point contact.

Perhaps the biggest problem today in galloping and jumping horses (as well as in dressage) is the misunderstanding of the upper body. The upper body should change with the gaits of the horse to not be either ahead or behind the motion. While behind the motion is more popular today and is not wrong (ahead of the

212

motion is wrong), it's way overdone.

But riders must know how to lean forward—by bending at the hips, closing the hip angle. Riders who lean forward at the shoulder will jut their heads and "roach" their backs.

At the standstill and while backing a horse, the upper body remains vertical to the ground. While walking, sitting the trot, and cantering, there should be a slight inclination forward, about 5 degrees. For galloping and jumping with the motion and for the posting trot, the inclination forward is about 30 degrees, the hip angle is well closed, the loins hollow, and the back flat.

Remember that while posting and jumping behind the motion is not wrong—and is sometimes right—it's rarely as smooth or effortless as riding with the motion. Most of our best grand prix riders ride with the motion but can instantly get behind.

Telling people to "sit up," as so many trainers do, is very dangerous. It puts riders unnecessarily behind the motion too much of the time and for no good reason. It does not balance the horse. Riders who are habitually behind on the approach usually have to catch up to the horse in the air. Catching up teaches them to duck over, jump ahead, or drop back in the air—all serious riding faults. Most riders at Harrisburg, even some of the best, demonstrated these flaws. Gordon Wright called it "excess motion."

The horse's motion should open the rider's knee angle and close the hip angle, while the ankle angle always stays closed. The rider should do nothing—the horse does the jumping, not the rider. Acrobatic jumping is something we want to discourage.

The long release of the hands halfway up the crest of the neck is an elementary technique. The short release, an inch or two up the neck, is an intermediate technique. Jumping out of hand, or the automatic release, is an advanced technique of the hands.

Not one finalist demonstrated the ability to be completely independent with the hands and maintain soft contact, with a straight line from elbow to mouth while jumping. The automatic release, with the exception of a handful of American Olympic riders, is extinct! And this is a shame because so many problems over big fences can only be solved by hand-to-mouth contact in the air. De Nemethy used to say, "Keep the connection!"

The crest release is also often done with a rotation or lift of the hands as the horse leaves the ground. This serious fault raises the horse's head and hollows his back. When using a crest release, the hands must rest and press on the crest of the horse's neck. They must push down, *never* pull back.

A lot of judges are most forgiving of this cardinal sin. We must get back to this automatic release for advanced jumping. We are the only country that demonstrates and exaggerates this often faulty crest release.

On the subject of hands, to repeat Bill Steinkraus' remark while the watching the ASPCA Maclay Finals several years ago, he said, "Why are all of the riders riding in handcuffs this year?" In other words, hands together are nice until one has to steer a horse. And then it becomes necessary to use the opening (leading) rein. The course at this year's Medal Finals demanded the opening rein. That's why so many

"Style comes first because it's even more fundamental."

"Without form, function is bound to deteriorate."

214

people had problems executing the sharp angles and turns.

Some readers may call this column negative and critical, but I feel it's necessary. I was disappointed in the style I saw, especially since these riders are our future team riders, professionals and teachers. I was always taught that good form on a horse comes first, like learning your ABCs. Without form, function is bound to deteriorate.

When I travel and teach in other countries, our affected, mannered and artificial techniques become more obvious. Yes, we do have the best base, but it's up to us teachers and judges to protect it.

40

In Pursuit Of The Elusive Feeling Of "Round"

January 2, 1998

Most riders whom I run across today—no matter where they live, no matter how young or old, no matter their experience on horseback, from pony riders to grand prix—are all trying to get their horses "round."

It wasn't always this way. Years ago, only the most sophisticated—Bill Steinkraus, Bert de Nemethy, Gabor Foltenyi—even knew what the word "round" meant. The rest of us went our merry ways, with our horses actually hollow and a bit stiff. And we were oblivious to the fact.

In many ways, those innocent days of old were better. For there is nothing worse than what I often see today—people who don't understand "round" trying to do something they do not understand in all the wrong ways.

In the hunter/jumper world, the most common mistake in trying to get a horse "round" is the use of ancillary reins (draw reins, gogues). I also see martingales adjusted too tight and all kinds of special bits and hackamores.

Usually, all that the riders accomplish is the shortening of the horse's neck, the lengthening out behind of the hindquarters, atrophied muscles, and compounded mouth problems.

I also see in this vain attempt at false roundness hands that are too low and wide (breaking the line below the mouth), and hands that saw the bit. These are very serious flaws in riders' hands and will eventually cause other even bigger problems in the riders' position and function on horseback.

"Roundness" is really a study only for the advanced pupil, but it's being thrown at everybody, even beginners. It's impossible to even approach this subject with someone before they have what I call educated hands, hands that resist the horse's mouth in exact proportion to the horse's resistance.

Good hands (versus bad hands or no hands) should be within reach of every rider; educated hands are something only a few ever achieve.

I don't even mention "roundness" or flexion until a rider has reached the Medal/Maclay level. And even then it's a real teaching/learning task. I spent 15 to 20 years in the saddle before I could properly "put a horse together" and "put him on the aids."

I really do long for the days when riders knew how to establish contact, close their legs, and put their horse up into their hands, just enough so that the horses and ponies carried them forward and to their fences.

Most of the time, "roundness" and flexion are the proverbial razors in the hands of monkeys.

I only work horses in plain snaffles and figure-eight nosebands. I'll jump and show horses in whatever makes them lightest. I like to ride jumpers in nosebands (hunters can't use anything but a plain cavesson) because all horses open their mouths to some degree, causing the lower jaw to resist the hand even more. I also like properly adjusted martingales, standing on hunters, running on jumpers (as per FEI rules).

"Round" means the whole horse, from his hind feet all the way up across his back, through the poll, to his nose. "Round" does not mean simply an arched neck and the horse's face on or behind the vertical.

The beginning of "round" comes when the rider settles softly into the saddle, picks up the reins, and puts their lower leg on the horse. He or she has then established contact, not just with both hands, but also with both legs and both seat bones. The horse is ready to be progressively and systematically enclosed by the rider's natural aids—legs, seat and hands. It's from varying degrees of pressure from these natural aids that one makes the horse truly "round."

The first thing one does after establishing contact is to teach the lesson of the legs. The horse must be taught, often through the artificial aids of the spur and the whip, to move instantly forward from the lightest closing of the legs into steady, receiving hands. This is the French "mise en main," the very first step of "round." This stage must never be forgotten. It is respected thousands of times each ride. It is also called "leg to hand."

It is most important to remember that while both legs drive the horse forward (creating impulsion), the inside leg is dominant. And while both hands regulate the impulsion, the outside hand is dominant (for the half-halt). The horse is more or less controlled by the diagonal frame from inside leg to outside hand.

The rider's legs and the horse's impulsion start and always maintain "roundness." Active, energetic hind legs that go higher and not faster produce engagement, or the bringing of the hind legs under the horse's mass. In turn, the horse raises his back progressively into the rider's seat, and only then is the horse able to lower his neck from the withers into the rider's receiving hands. This is called descent of the neck.

Once the horse is truly going from leg to hand, the *sine qua non* of "roundness," it's up to the hands by closing the fingers (the fixed hand), half-halts, subtle vibrations (sliding the bit), and flexions (direct or lateral) to place the horse's head.

All of the hand actions are difficult to do right. They are, to be perfectly frank, only for advanced riders.

While the outside rein is primarily responsible for regulating the impulsion through half-halts, the inside rein is more responsible for flexions of the mouth. Flexion occurs when the horse yields his jaw to one rein (lateral flexion) or both reins (direct flexion).

During a lateral flexion, the horse's head and upper neck yield down to the side. During a direct flexion, the horse brings his nose straight down. Lateral flexion is apparent during all lateral schooling exercises and while cantering. Direct flexion should be a part of transitions and longitudinal schooling exercises.

The shoulder-in is the most important exercise in training a horse because it accomplishes so

"Educated hands are something only a few ever achieve."

"Most of the time, 'roundness' and flexion are the proverbial razors in the hands of monkeys."

219

many things: inside leg to outside hand, bending, straightness, suppleness, engagement, and (perhaps most importantly) submission to the hand and leg on the same side (lateral aids), to which no horse can resist.

The shoulder-in, shoulder-out, haunches-in (travers), haunches-out (renvers) and half-pass render the horse to the aids. All of these lateral exercises on two tracks, as well as all lateral exercises on one track, ask the horse to bend around the inside leg.

These exercises produce "roundness" from the inside leg to the outside hand, not from the hands alone.

The longitudinal suppling exercises, transitions within gaits and from one gait to another only confirm the basic theory. By constantly making transitions, the hands and legs work closer and closer together. Finally, they almost contradict each other, and "roundness" occurs.

This is yet a different theory: 4 pounds of legs, 1 pound of hand in forward transitions; 4 pounds of hands, 1 pound of leg in backward transitions.

Christilot Boylen, the Canadian dressage rider, says that the horse must always be "in front of the legs and behind the hands" (not behind the bit), and she is right.

A correctly "round" horse feels very energetic behind, up in his back into the rider's seat, and round, and soft and steady in the hand. A correctly schooled horse should stay this way during all forward and backward transitions and during any exercise.

Of course, this is much easier said than done, and it's a life-long quest. Of all the great grand prix jumping riders in the world, probably only a handful could get on almost any horse in just a snaffle and in minutes make him truly round in all his gaits.

It's a challenge such as this that makes me get up in the morning, even though we can never conquer the whole spectrum of horsemanship.

Jimmy Williams once said to me, "You know, George, it's what you learn after you think you know it all that really counts."

As usual, Jimmy was right.

41

The Evolution Of Style

November 12, 1999

I've always been a devotee of and have had a passionate interest in styles of riding. How one sits a horse has always intrigued me. Probably because I was not the most natural of riders, I had to use my intellect and work on my own style in order to succeed at all.

Style not only enables a rider to sit more securely and gives him better balance while riding and jumping a horse, but good position also enables him to communicate better with his horse by correct use of his aids.

Probably the greatest virtue of good style is its benefit to the horse. *Good style always makes it easier and more comfortable for the horse.* This is especially true when understanding the sensitivity and the extreme delicateness of the horse's mouth and back!

As a rule, I'm disappointed in people's style, or, rather, lack of style. Fortunately, there are some stylists in every discipline to keep the faith. Anky van Grunsven, Robert Dover and Christine Traurig in dressage; David O'Connor and Mark Todd in eventing;

Michael Matz, Joe Fargis, Rodrigo Pessoa, Anne Kursinski, Ian Millar, Beezie Madden, Hap Hansen and Susie Hutchison in show jumping; and Emily Williams, our 1999 AHSA Medal winner, in equitation.

While judging the AHSA Medal Finals, Sue Ashe and I believed only a few possessed classic style. This isn't to say that many didn't ride well and get the job done.

There appear to be four basic and historic styles of riding in the world: English, German, French and Italian. The American style could now be considered a fifth. It's stood on its own for quite a long time. But, actually, the American style evolved this century as a combination/blend of the four basic European styles.

Because we were once a colony of England, we were most influenced initially by English horsemanship. In fact, all the countries originally connected to England either geographically (Scotland, Ireland, Wales) or politically (South Africa, Canada, Australia, New Zealand, India, Hong Kong, etc.) rode the English way.

The English seat evolved from necessity, practicality and survival. Years ago, English equitation was strictly cross-country equitation, foxhunting to be specific. And riding in pursuit of hounds took place over uneven terrain and over many different types of obstacles (banks, ditches, hedges, wall, gates, rails and other "fly" fences).

So riders developed a practical response: sometimes they rode a little long, sometimes very short, their stirrups were invariably "thrust" home on their foot, they gripped strongly with their knees, sometimes they stood up to gallop, but often sat down on the back of their saddles with a "roach" back. The English used the Pelham or double bridle, which was successful on a variety

223

of breeds and types of horses.

When I started riding in the late 1940s and early '50s, this was called the English hunting seat. It was still used in the show rings then, and people could and did win equitation classes riding that way. Now, this way of riding is extinct, unless you stumble upon it in the hunting field.

The Italian seat evolved from the Italians' love of the Thoroughbred and through their good fortune of having a countryman named Federico Caprilli.

Caprilli (who lived about a hundred years ago) probably did more for riding and for the horse, around the world, than any man in history did.

Virtually every riding nation in the world at that time sent representatives and emissaries to Italy to study Caprilli's techniques, which they took home with them. And each country adopted and interpreted his philosophy in their own way and incorporated these ideas into their own existing system. It worked for the whole world!

Caprilli revolutionized riding, racing and jumping. In general, he wanted to make life easier for the race horse, cross-country horse and the jumping horse. And he did. Horses went faster and jumped better under riders who adopted his techniques.

Caprilli shortened stirrups, kept the foot home in the stirrup, kept the grip in the knees, and got riders leaning forward, off their horses' backs. He advocated following the gestures of the horse's head and neck, both on the ground and over fences, with soft, giving hands and arms. In other words, Caprilli "liberated" the muscles in the head, neck, back and limbs of the horse so that he could do his job.

The French, in their love of beauty, bring style to everything they touch. Over the centuries, they have bisected, dissected and analyzed style on horseback more than any other school, save perhaps our own.

They discovered the best leg on a horse, with the stirrup on the ball of the foot, the heels down and in, the ankles relaxed, the grip *below* the knee, in the calf of the leg.

They understood that the posture on a horse changed according to the speeds one was traveling, as well as the job that was being done. They understood the importance of hands and that a straight line from rider's elbow to horse's mouth made all the difference in developing a good mouth and good hands.

The French school spread far and wide through the first half of the century, yet not so much now. The French-speaking parts of Switzerland and Belgium, as well as Luxembourg and northern Spain, use French riding a good deal. Due to James Fillis' long residence in the court of in Russia early in the century, the French influenced the Russian school too. You can see Fillis in their dressage riders even today.

The country that received the most from the French has been ours. Before World Wars I and II, cavalry officers were sent abroad to the great schools of Europe to study and to bring home their ideas. It appears that the greatest influence came from the French and the Italians. This is probably because we always enjoyed cross–country equitation, hacking, foxhunting, racing and showing a bit more than dressage. These two schools of thought also suited our often-hot Thoroughbred horses.

The German school of riding has emerged as the most powerful influence in the world today. Why? Simply because they're winning. And why are they winning? I believe it has more to do with their single-minded mentality and work ethic than with their techniques and methodology.

The German school (which also includes the Dutch, parts

of Switzerland and Belgium, Austria, Spain in a sense, Eastern Europe and Scandinavia) is based almost exclusively on dressage, ring riding and control. Turning horses out in paddocks, trail riding, foxhunting, hacking, getting off a horse's mouth and back are not first and foremost in their minds. They are a dominating people and have developed breeds of horses that require domination.

This is in no way criticizing the Germans. They are great horsemen and have won the most. Although I'm mostly German/Dutch in ancestry and think and act very German, I'm French/Italian in my thinking about horses.

The German style evolved from the type of heavy horses they bred, their confined space to ride in, and their necessity to control. That, to some extent, is why they almost always sit down in the saddle.

Their position details a strong knee grip, toes parallel, the lower legs movable to some degree, the seat always deep, the toes almost always low, and the hands low, while the upper body remains erect at all times. The Dutch ride even deeper than the Germans.

Modern dressage and all its confines suit the Germans and the Dutch today more than it does other peoples. I remember riding with the legendary Danish master Gunnar Anderson. Twice a week, aboard Jessica Newberry Ransehausen's Grand Prix dressage horses, he would jack up his stirrups four holes and jump them over solid logs and walls cross-country. He said it was good for their backs and their minds. I doubt this kind of thing happens too often now.

The American style, which includes Canada, Mexico and to some degree all of Central and South America, evolved last and from these four basic European styles.

226

As I've said, the fundamental base ingredient of our style comes from England. It was then refined by the Italian influences, the French schools, and through our own cavalry and their representatives, such as Gordon Wright, Jimmy Williams, Vladimir Littauer, Jane Marshall Dillon, Bill Steinkraus and Raymond Burr. This recipe of ideas and techniques not only suited our jumpers, but it also suited the hunters and the equitation divisions.

"Caprilli probably did more for riding and for the horse, around the world, than any man in history did."

Since the mid-1950s, there's been an increasingly stronger influence by the German school, namely Bert de Nemethy, Richard Watjen and Gabor Foltenyi, just to name a few. The influence today is more from self-taught European competitors and horse dealers.

Now a universal style is evolving. Through air travel, people from throughout the world are mingling, showing, training and dealing together daily. The world is smaller, and there are no boundaries.

"Probably the greatest virtue of good style is its benefit to the horse."

While there's still a recognizable identity between riders from different countries, it's much less than in the past. We're all beginning to look more alike.

While this is good in one way, it's bad in another. I used to enjoy (in dressage especially) watching the distinct differences in position and riding techniques from country to country.

In judging, watching and analyzing the riding in the AHSA Medal Finals, I was nostalgic for a

227

purer, more attractive American style of years ago. As long as the teachers are compelled to put their students behind the motion of the horse, most, if not all, of the time (often with longer stirrups), there will be faults. There will be heels up, looseness, sitting on the buttocks rather than the crotch, stiffness, roached backs, dropping back in the air, ducking and jumping ahead of the horse. These form faults happened regularly at the Pennsylvania National.

It's not really the teachers' fault, yet they're responsible. There is so much information (often contradictory) being thrown around at people today that it's hard to decipher what's necessary. Using the grading system works best for me. Teach people only what they need to know for their level of riding.

And keep riding beautifully.

42

Style Is A Missing Ingredient In Younger Riders

March 10, 2000

Once again, watching the grand prix classes this year in Florida has brought home to me the importance of form over fences in relation to function.

Some people will be disappointed to hear this, but the best riders we have are of an older generation.

These riders were so indoctrinated by the basics of good, old-fashioned American horsemanship, including good form on a horse, that they've never forgotten it. Michael Matz, Joe Fargis, Katie Prudent, Beezie Madden, Anne Kursinski, Leslie Howard and Norman Dello Joio are few who come to mind on the East Coast. Hap Hansen, Francie Steinwedell-Carvin and Susie Hutchison would be a few examples on the West Coast.

Yes, we have a newer generation of good, younger riders. They most certainly get the job done and win. However, the whole picture is rare to see today.

First, when considering style, look at the horse. A horse in good condition, the proper weight, a gloss to his coat, properly clipped, trimmed and braided (the American braid job, please!) is what we want to see in any show ring. Today, corners are often cut in this department. Michael Matz' presentation on any of his horses represents the epitome of turn-out. It's called spit and polish.

Now, to examine the rider: The rider's body is divided into four parts—the leg, back, upper body and hands and arms. Equilibrium is, in a sense, a fifth part. When the four parts work correctly, the rider is secure and in balance. When a part is out of whack, balance and security are lost to a degree.

Most people today in the grand prix world have and understand an educated leg. There are really only two positions for the leg. One is at the back edge of the girth, and the other is slightly farther back, say a hand's width.

Using the leg in front of the girth on a horse's shoulder is a third position, but we rarely use it in jumping a horse—perhaps in training. But the position is a bit complicated and easily compromises balance.

Just about every jumping rider in the world agrees that the heels should be down, ankles flexed, and the toes out a shade, with the stirrup placed on the ball of the foot. Most people today have a lower-leg contact, not just the knee. "Kicking and booting" is now a thing of the past.

Extremes are never good in riding. There are three possibilities when riding a horse—be with him, ahead of him, or behind him. Being ahead of a horse's motion is never right. Being with him or behind him are both correct.

I like the old adage, "ride in the middle of your horse," neither too far back nor too far ahead. Excessive riding behind the horse, as is often seen today, cannot just be blamed on the European horse. I blame it on fashion and fad.

Anne, Katie and Michael school their horses to their lower leg (light to the leg) and teach their horses to carry them when riding with the motion. Of course, these riders are quick to get behind at a moment's notice when they need to. The best way to produce impulsion, of course, is with the legs and spurs. The seat is used more for support.

Galloping and jumping a horse is much the same as trotting. Sitting the trot or sitting the gallop adds to the rider's strength and security. However, it loads the horse's back and is harder for the horse and rider.

Posting the trot and standing slightly at the gallop, while it might diminish the rider's strength, makes it easier and lighter for both horse and rider. That's why we teach two ways to trot (posting and sitting) and two ways to gallop (full seat and light seat, or three-point and two-point contact). Both are necessary.

Style over fences, in my opinion, has been compromised greatly by the ridiculous and excessive sitting down to the point that it crushes the horse's back, hollows his back, and most certainly affects the hind legs, both on the flat and over fences. Many horses today jump with flat backs and hit fences behind.

With, behind and ahead of the horse's motion have to do with the rider's upper body, the third part of the equation. A rider positions the upper body in relation to the vertical line to the ground, according to the job being done and the gait being ridden.

There should be a great change of position in the upper body, from the vertical, to occasionally behind the vertical, to the racing position—inclined forward over the horse's neck. While great riders can shift their positions instantaneously, the medium position for posting, galloping and jumping should be about 30 degrees in front of the vertical. Spending most of the time riding in this position makes it easier for both horse and rider.

Of course hot, light, sensitive Thoroughbred horses require riders to keep a light, soft seat and more of an inclination forward of the upper body. Unfortunately, we don't have enough of this kind of horse around today. About 80 percent of the horses we see today are of the more phlegmatic middle- or heavyweight type. The European warmblood has for the most part replaced the American Thoroughbred.

As a rule, the riders of great style have a more forward inclination of the upper body at all gaits and, consequently, a softer, lighter seat.

In discussing hands and arms, the fourth part of the rider's body, it's best (as with the rest of the rider's position) to stay strict by definition. The rider must maintain a straight line from his elbow to the horse's mouth. Hands should be over and in front of the horse's withers, a couple of inches apart, with the thumbs just inside the vertical.

Today, many riders in the jumper ring have long reins, which entice the rider's upper body and seat to go still farther back behind the motion. Years ago, we used to call it riding "by the seat of the pants." Today, it appears, we have legitimized this seat-of-the-pants position.

Very long reins, very short reins, too low hands, and too high hands are all exaggerations. They don't look good or work well. And by being in an incorrect position, other parts of the body are affected. For instance, hands too low pull down on the shoulders and tend to give a rider a "roached" back. Too short a rein can put a rider ahead of the motion, just as too long a rein can put a rider too far behind the motion.

Most people use their eyes excellently. First, they've been taught to use their eyes correctly. And, second, they don't foxhunt. Many people who used to come to the show ring from the hunting field were in the habit of looking down—probably for holes!

And what's happened to invisible aids? Katie Prudent's riding down here in Florida on her mare Belladonna is living proof that invisible aids—aids used with such discretion that one cannot see what's going on—still exist.

The acrobatics on horseback, as well as the rough-and-ready school of horsemanship, are not pretty sights to behold. When I think of our successes during the 1960s, '70s and '80s and the style in which we achieved those successes, I must say our attention to this detail has diminished considerably.

Now, often the name of the game is to get it done, no matter how or what it looks like. Riding, to me, has always been much more than that. And I salute those who still keep those ideals in sight. Win, yes, but do it with style and class.

43

Why Could So Few Juniors Answer The Questions Our Course Asked?

November 1, 2002

Last spring, Kip Rosenthal, my old friend and student who had asked me to co-judge with her at the [USEF] Medal Finals, showed me the course she wanted to use for the finals. I took one look and told her it was "a stroke of genius."

There were seven fences, all of which had to be ridden "off the rider's eye." There were no mechanically numbered lines. On paper, this course looked ridiculously simple. To execute it well in actual competition under pressure was a different matter.

On Saturday afternoon before the championships, Kip and I looked over Steve Stephens' beautiful jump material. We used all short standards, deep cups, and natural-type obstacles found in the hunting field. Of course, the horses and riders were not used to this look, and that alone was to cause a very big problem.

Kip and I arrived at 5 a.m. to set the course. Craig Bergman and his trusty jump crew were right on the job. Since there were only seven individual fences to construct, we were set up a full

45 minutes before the riders and trainers were allowed to walk the course.

Fence 1, a 3'6" brush box without wings, was situated on the quarter line, in the middle of the long side, directly opposite the judges' stand. Fences 2 and 3 were next to fence 1, on the same line, so that riders had to basically ride a serpentine to jump them.

Fence 2 was a beautifully varnished, light brown chicken coop with a rail on top. There were small trees alongside acting as a frame. The turn to this fence had an easy option—going inside the last fence, a triple bar of walls set on the diagonal. Everyone practiced this shortish turn.

Fence 3, alongside the rail on the far side of the ring, was a hogsback made out of three brown rails and straw bales. It was about 4'7" wide, which beautifully prepared the horses for the upcoming oxer combination.

Fences 4A and 4B, directly across the ring, right under the judges' box, were identical oxers. Each fence was comprised of six varnished split rails, 3'6" high and 4' wide.

Fence 5, after a right turn, was a narrow garden gate without wings, perpendicular to the first four fences and about 20 feet off the middle of the short side. The placement of the fence allowed riders an option turn: they could either make a half-turn to the right or a half-turn in reverse to the left into the wall after jumping. Most turned left, although some turned right.

Fences 6A and 6B were the oxer combination in the other direction. Fences 7, 8 and 9 were the reverse direction of fences 3, 2 and 1. And fence 10 was the triple bar on the diagonal toward the out-gate. Craig designed this attractive fence out of three small stonewalls and colorful flowers.

Every fence caused some problems, even the brush, because it wasn't framed with some sort of wing, unlike the jumps in every other equitation course you see today.

The two *big* problems, of course, were the double of oxers and the narrow garden gate. Mind you, the oxers were only 35'6" apart, and they were only 3'6" high and 4' wide. In my experience, I would not call this a huge scope test. In hindsight, though, I believe that the light on the varnished rails made the "look" of this combination much harder than we'd anticipated. Also, many people rode it badly. Why would you make a jump-off turn to the scopey combination with no impulsion and no distance? Believe me, many did just that!

It appeared to Kip and me that many riders were locked into counting a certain number of strides between the combination and the garden gate, so there were many run-outs. For most, it was better to ride it on a very straight line as a fence by itself.

The two girls that we had on top after the morning round were each stylists whom we both liked. They each galloped to the first fence in a forward seat, just as you would do to such a fence across country. Each made beautiful, prompt turns to fences 2 and 3 and did it again going back on these fences as numbers 7, 8 and 9.

Maggie Jayne made especially "handy" turns, but both she and Tedra Bates used great judgment to the combination in both directions. They had enough pace (impulsion), gave themselves enough room, and found beautiful, accurate distances. They rode just strongly enough. So many riders either rode "chicken" to the in-and-out or over-rode, attacking it and knocking it down.

After this testing combination, both girls took their time, kept their horses between hand and leg, and jumped the garden gate without risking a run-out.

For the last fence, they stepped on the gas and, maintaining their beautiful style, demonstrated how to jump out of pace.

The rules require the judges to call back between 20 and 25 riders. We called back 22, those who had scores of 85 or higher. Maggie and Tedra were the only ones who broke 90. It surprised me. I thought we'd have more.

"Perhaps this class was a hard, much-needed wake-up call."

For the second round, we kept all the fences in place, except for reversing the triple bar. This course came up quicker, and more of the fences were related in the number of strides. It proved to be just right for the afternoon course, but there were lots of minor problems.

Again, Maggie's ride proved to be the best, and her score even improved a point.

And, of course, it's mandatory to test at least the top four contestants. We called in our top four, asked them to work collectively on the flat and then to halt. Maggie Jayne had proven, not only to us, but also to anyone watching, that this was unquestionably her championship for the taking. Why risk her losing it with some complicated ride-off? That wouldn't have been fair.

"Jumping in this country has become too mechanical, too stereotyped."

In hindsight, I'll admit that parts of this course proved much harder than Kip or I had anticipated. But there is another side of the coin. Perhaps this class was a hard, much-need wake-up call. I'll guarantee that 20, 30 or even 40 years ago there wouldn't have been as many problems as we saw this time.

Riding and jumping in this country today have become too soft, too mechanical, and too stereotyped. Teachers and trainers must give their riders the opportunity to practice courage, practice variety, practice judgment. If they only go from show to show to show, riders never have to address these factors.

Could some of these same weaknesses be affecting our Olympic-level show jumpers? Yes, probably.

Don't forget, our great Olympic medalists (Bill Steinkraus, Frank Chapot, Mary Chapot, Joe Fargis, Conrad Homfeld and Leslie Howard) most always came out of the Medal/Maclay ranks. The equitation division was always intended to make riders and horsemen, not robots. Let's remember the intent and get back to that mission.

44

This Is What Form Over Fences Looks Like

January 7, 2005

Last month (and long before!) I was thumbing through issues of the *Chronicle*, and I was truly appalled by the style—or lack of style—of the top professional hunter riders in this country. Yes, I'm sure they have a great feel, sense of pace, and eye for a distance, but, my fellow horsemen, that is not enough!

In years gone by, we didn't have videotapes. Yes, home movies (sometimes even in slow motion) were fairly popular. So what we counted on were the still photographs taken by the great horse show photographers of that day.

Victor Hugo-Vidal, Ronnie Mutch and I would pore over our photos after every show, from both the equitation and the hunter classes. We'd be mortified if our heel was up, leg too far back, eyes down, if we were ducking over, or if we were not maintaining a straight line from elbow to the horse's mouth.

If I had a really decent picture, I'd take it to my teacher Gordon Wright. Or later, once I'd made the U.S. Equestrian Team, to Bert de Nemethy or Bill Steinkraus. Billy was particularly "picky," and I liked that. He controlled his riding position down to his little finger.

In desperation over our current plight, I called John Strassburger, the *Chronicle's* editor, to ask him to dig up some photos from the 1950s so we could compare then and now. We will present six photos, one an international amateur, one an amateur woman, one junior, and three outstanding professionals of the day for you. After that, you can go back the last few months (or years, for that matter) and compare. I'm sure you'll agree that, although much is better in our sport, style and position are worse.

I understand that some riders think that today's fences are bigger and tougher than they were in the old days. Wrong. First of all, those fences were much bigger. And, second, all of today's fences are ascending, triple-bar type fences. Anyone who jumps knows the simplest fences are those ascending fences.

The fences you see in these photos were all vertical or nearly vertical, with little if any groundlines, and they were solid. And they were big—4 feet and more.

Photo No. 1 is somebody you all know. Frank Chapot was a six-time Olympian and won the individual bronze medal at the 1974 World Championships, to touch on just a few of his accomplishments. There was no kind of class that Frank could not win. He won the ASPCA Maclay Finals, was AHSA Working Hunter Champion of the year, and won nearly all the jumper classes at one time or another, both here and abroad.

Here Frank is pictured aboard Peggy Augustus' champion working hunter Defense at the Cologne (Germany) show in 1956. Yes, not infrequently, some of our great hunters went to Europe and stepped up to the jumper classes like this. Can you imagine that happening today?

Actually this could be a tall hunter type of fence. The horse is in great form—and so is the rider. Frank's leg is anchored down with the weight in his heels. His seat has cleared the saddle, neither jumping ahead nor dropping back. His upper body is parallel to that of the horse. Eyes up. And almost a perfectly straight line from elbow to mouth. Although the style of the day was to have more foot in the stirrup than today, I consider this a great picture of style over fences.

Carol Weber Del Guercio **(Photo No. 2)** was a lovely amateur rider who handily jumped the 4'6" courses of the day. After all, there weren't any amateur-owner classes. They had amateur ladies and gentleman's classes in the open hunter divisions. Period.

Carol's mount here is Fairview Farms' legendary seal-brown gelding Bronze Wing. To be perfectly honest, I best remember this horse under Betty Bosley. Bronze Wing was a beautiful Thoroughbred horse, a "10" mover, and a scopey jumper. He did not have the tightest front end, but he had a good front end.

Carol is in good form here. Perhaps her stirrup is back on her foot and her leg a touch too far forward. This, of course, has caused her seat to slip too far to the rear. Her eyes are up, her posture excellent, and she's showing a beautiful and correct "short" release.

New York's Madison Square Garden (the only real National Horse Show in my book!) looks pretty good here too, in 1956. Notice the elegance of the judges, spectators and jump crew in the background. And note the simplicity and vertical construction of these true hunter fences. Oh, I have such nostalgia!

241

photo 1 **Frank Chapot**

photo 2 **Carol Werber Del Guercio**

242

photo 3 **Peter Winkelman**

photo 4 **Bobby Barker**

243

photo 5 **Raymond Burr**

photo 6 **Cappy Smith**

244

Photo No. 3 shows Peter Winkelman aboard his own great-performing junior and working hunter champion Little Trip over the big hedge at Fairfield, Conn. This hedge was about 4'10" high and at least 5 feet wide—see what I mean about how big these jumps were?

Unfortunately, the photo is a fraction late and doesn't do the horse justice. But look at Peter and his near-perfect position. Again, in those days we rode with the stirrup truly back on the ball of the foot. (Rodney Jenkins probably brought us nearer to the toe!) And he is outgrowing his boots. So what! Boots are expensive.

Peter is "tight as a tick," his heels are down, his seat just out of the saddle, eyes up, and a perfectly relaxed yet straight back. Peter has a beautiful "automatic" release with a straight line from elbow to mouth. This is form over fences!

Photo No. 4 is none other than legendary horseman Bobby Burke. Bobby is not only one of the great horsemen of the last 50 years, but also one of its most colorful personalities.

This photo is vintage "Burkie." He rode with his foot close to "home" in the stirrup and cocked his toe a little bit in front of him. Note the tight leg grip and the exemplary seat position just clear of the saddle. Bobby's eyes and head are up, with his posture soft and relaxed. Bobby also rode with a bit of a longer rein and a "short" release all the time. This is where he put his hands, but he never "stiffed" his horses.

The Tyrolean hat was often part of Bobby's "look," as was the handkerchief in his hip pocket. We all tried to copy him.

Although the horse is jumping a bit over his front end, he's very attractive and magnificently turned out. Everything about "Burkie" and his horses was classy and stylish.

This is a real hunter fence without the over-abundance of groundlines that we see today.

Raymond Burr, Emerson Burr's brother (**in Photo No. 5**), was probably the greatest stylist of his era or any era. His angles were so correct that the great artist Paul Brown used him as an example for his drawings.

Yes, it was a hot and dusty day at the Fairfield (Conn.) Hunt Club. Raymond always rode a number of horses, and his boots are dusty. So what! Look at his angles on horseback. His ankle angle has stayed closed, his knee angle has opened just enough, his hips are closed, and the angle in his elbow affords him just that perfect straight line from elbow to mouth. Raymond's eyes are up, and he always had impeccable posture on a horse.

Raymond is a study in form over fences. He usually rode with his stirrup a bit back and held quite a short curb rein above the snaffle, between his second and third finger. He will be best remembered as a rider for his position, smoothness and incredible eye for a distance. No matter how fast–and he really galloped on those outside courses–he never came wrong to a fence. And he rarely wore a hat.

Morton W. "Cappy" Smith (**Photo No. 6**) was another giant in his field, bigger than life. Cappy was more than 6 feet tall, had movie-star looks and a personality to go with it, and was a great, great horseman.

His position here exemplifies the forward seat—heels down, ankles flexed, toes out, legs in contact, seat slightly out of the saddle, back flat, eyes up, and a perfectly straight line with light contact to the horse's mouth. I don't see riders like this in the hunter ring today.

This photo was taken at the Upperville show in Virginia. I remember the horse Jazz Session very well, especially as a green horse. He was a very pretty horse and always won the model and the hack classes. Being a bit of a limited jumper, as you can see by his hind end, Cappy would always "nurse" him around, getting him called back in the top three or four. Because of his conformation and Cappy's showmanship, the horse usually ended up on top, especially as a 3'6" horse.

I hope you have enjoyed turning back the clock with these six wonderful photos as much as I have. History is a great teacher. And we mustn't forget these days—when perhaps some things were better.

As you all know, I am a great proponent of the forward seat as taught by Caprilli, Chamberlin, Wright, Steinkraus, Littauer, Williams and de Nemethy. We must protect this way of riding for the good of the galloping, jumping horse, as well as for riders of future generations. Professionals are our role models, so it is especially important that they exemplify this classic way of riding. 🐎

George,
On Tour

Tricia Booker photo

45

The Horse Scene In The Soviet Union

September 7, 1990

Several years ago some Soviet trainers attended my annual clinic in Helsinki, Finland, and a trip to the Soviet Union started to evolve.

When issuing this rather informal invitation, the Soviets were very clear: They didn't want a clinic as such—something I am very accustomed to doing all over the world—but rather they wanted to show me around the horse facilities, and I would conduct a few lectures at seminars. How this would differ from my normal teaching-training format remained to be seen.

August 1990 seemed the ideal moment to go. The World Equestrian Games would be over; Stockholm is relatively convenient to Moscow; and the weather would probably be warm—not cold!

I boarded Scandinavian Airlines bound for Moscow and, I believed, probably one of the more interesting ventures of my life with horses, a life that's already been packed with thrills, spills and chills.

It did take an hour for the luggage to arrive and another hour to stand in line going through customs. So what? That's travel. It was a great relief to walk through and see my name on a small sign held by an American-looking and sounding, attractive young woman named Helen, who soon told me she was my "keeper."

We got in a car with a driver. Soon I became impressed: very wide, clear avenues and massive apartment buildings, beautiful architecture, not only of the very old but also of the Stalinist era of the 1950s. Red Square, the Kremlin, old palaces and parks were all gorgeous beyond description. I'd heard Moscow was drab. I totally disagree.

After crossing the center of the city, we arrived at my abode, the Sports Hotel. It seems to house athletes from all over the world. The food is not *tour d'argent*, but it's OK. Nobody seems to sleep, though. Between the traffic and the radios blaring, sleep is secondary. My spit-and-polish boots, spurs, breeches, and hunt cap were definitely not the norm in the Olympic village-type atmosphere of the Sports Hotel. Running shoes, shorts and T-shirts were what to wear. Anyway, I survived the curious glances, had breakfast, and was met by Oleg Ovodov and company. Ovodov is a Russian chef d'equipe, and we had met before at various horse shows around the world.

We headed out to the Military Riding Club. It seems all of the equestrian centers are called clubs. Iwan Kalita is head of this club. I remember him well riding Tarif back in the 1972 Munich Games to a dressage team gold medal.

After showing us the impressive facilities, which included several good-sized indoor rings, an underground tunnel (used as protection against the Russian winters—connected to stabling for several hundred horses), a veterinary clinic, tennis courts, a gym, shooting and fencing areas, we headed toward a large

251

outdoor sand ring full of jumps.

Mr. Kalita soon asked me if I wanted a ride, and I said sure, picking a steady-looking 9-year-old. I figured I didn't need to show the Russians how well I could fall off a young, green, playful stallion.

"I'd heard Moscow was drab. I totally disagree."

Soon, being the compulsive teacher I am, I demonstrated to the young soldiers riding around with me some of our American techniques. We had in no time at all a very constructive and impromptu clinic going.

They all seemed pleased and fascinated to learn and to practice closing the hip angle, stirrup on the ball of the foot, contact in the lower leg, eyes up and focused on a point, the weight of the rider's hand and body resting on the horse's crest while jumping, the long release, the short release, and, most important of all, to wait for one's horse—not jump ahead. We all had fun, and they were very apt pupils.

"The whole city of Leningrad is a museum."

The director of the next club I visited was obviously a good horseman like Kalita. He showed me horse after horse of tremendous quality.

Most of the Russian horses are seven-eighths, if not completely, Thoroughbred. They have beautiful, refined heads, delicate nostrils, thin skin and bulging brown eyes. As a type, they are definitely in the class of our own American Thoroughbred.

The next day we went to the equestrian facility built for the 1980 Moscow Olympic games. Some of the points of interest were: a huge outdoor grass stadium containing a big water and a liverpool, an Olympic event course and a steeplechase track, a big outdoor sand ring with a good set of fences, a fascinating gallery housing photos of all Soviet equestrian Olympic winners of this century, and a very attractive lecture hall.

The group that I taught that day was definitely more sophisticated. They also were keen to learn and very athletic— definitely not fat and soft. We covered a lot more territory than the previous day, including upper-body positions at different gaits, shoulder-in, cavaletti to a vertical, stopping on a line, riding a broken line in six strides, heels down, and the use of the long release through a multiple in-and-out of four low oxers. The riders' tongues were hanging out after an hour and a half.

We went to the lecture hall for questions and answers. Funnily enough, there was another interpreter speaking Spanish. Lo and behold there was a Cuban trainer in the group.

The whole city of Leningrad is a museum. The Hermitage, Peter's Palace and Isaac's Cathedral are the tip of the iceberg. A Venice of the north, with all of its palaces, waterways and color, it has got to rank as one of the world's most beautiful cities.

The second day we drove out of town for about half an hour. It was raining quite hard. Suddenly we came upon a rather half- finished, dilapidated riding establishment in the middle of nowhere. Getting out of the car, who should be there but Iwan Kizimow. A veteran of four Olympic Games—Tokyo, Mexico, Munich, Montreal—this man has won countless gold and silver medals in championship competition. He was running a mock dressage competition for his juniors.

I couldn't believe it. There were these kids in their white breeches and dress coats, the rain pouring down, performing beautiful, light, active, accurate tests. We stood in a bus along the short side with the judges.

Too soon, I said goodbye to my Russian friends, thinking that my time spent in the Soviet Union proved to me that the horse can, indeed, supercede politics.

46

The Heroes Of Barcelona

September 4, 1992

Barcelona is a lively but extremely hot city situated right on the Mediterranean Sea, which is the only thing that makes the weather bearable. We all kept thinking how stressful this hot climate is on horses and that Atlanta, where the Olympics will be in four years, is nowhere near the coast.

It's a mystery to everyone why climactic conditions like this are inflicted upon humans and horses in Olympics after Olympics.

The Olympic venue, the Real Club de Polo, was most efficient, with excellent permanent stabling and more than enough practice areas. There was also a comfortable clubhouse with an air-conditioned bar (rare in Spain), and that gave it a special intimacy that made a big difference.

What wasn't fun was the inflexible, inconsistent tactics used by the rude personnel controlling the venue. They made it most unpleasant.

The main sand arena was perfect, and Nicholas Alvarez de Boorques did an excellent job with the courses, although many, many people disagreed with me on this.

For one thing, his courses looked stark. But Spain looks stark. There were no elaborate "designer" wings, and flowers and shrubbery were at a minimum. This bareness caused horses and riders to focus on the fences, and this was intimidating.

I would classify de Boorques as an old-fashioned course builder. He set many airy fences, wide fences, and careful fences. The construction of the individual jumps was, I thought, brilliant. Many seasoned, bold horses were surprised. His use of liverpools and water was excellent.

By using hunter-type distances that were 3 to 4 feet longer than normal, he made interesting distance problems in the lines. The time allowed provided a challenge because it was always tight, which was correct.

The "friendly" or warm-up competition showed us nothing. It only gave us a chance to get our horses into the ring. That course had no liverpool, no water and only one line with very simple related distances. I didn't think it was big, but some did.

One thing really impressed me: the course designer gave away none of his tricks.

The next two days were devoted to team dressage. The standard was excellent and the Germans outstanding. We Americans were elated to win the bronze medal. Carol Lavell and Gifted, and Jessica Ransehousen as chef d'equipe, were particularly responsible for this success. But the whole dressage community has really pulled together, which certainly hasn't been true of our show jumping and eventing efforts. We'd better start getting serious like the rest of the world if we want to win in Atlanta. We are often children at play; the Europeans are men at work.

The Nations Cup, even more than four years ago at Seoul, proved one thing—through education and association, equality in show jumping has spread throughout the world. Ten teams could have won. Almost everyone rides well, or at least adequately, today, and this trend is only going to continue.

The course for the Nations Cup was difficult but fair. The hard parts were the triple combination of oxer, vertical, oxer going away from the in-gate and with natural rails framed by bright green, solid standards; the tight double of verticals separated by two strides; and a very difficult liverpool with airy planks over it, again away from the in-gate. This last fence provided suspense right to the end of the course.

The Dutch win was no surprise, but the Austrians finishing second was a surprise in a way. They only had three riders get around the course. But in a way it was no surprise at all—they have Hugo Simon and Thomas Fruhmann. The French were predictably third, but I'm sure the Spanish were disappointed with their excellent fourth after all the time, effort and money they've spent getting ready for Barcelona in the hope of getting a medal.

Our tie for fifth, with Switzerland, was a decent showing, though not nearly good enough for a country with our record. The real shock was that the English and the Germans finished so far back. But that's show jumping.

The dressage battle of the century between Rembrandt and Gigolo came next. Nicole Uphoff's performance on Rembrandt was a demonstration why the Germans have won more medals in the Olympic Games than anyone else. They aren't afraid to take a chance. Uphoff didn't just ride a dressage test, she gave a demonstration. It was as good a ride as I'd ever seen.

257

The Friday individual show jumping qualifier was a big, big course. Unfortunately, the order was the reverse of the standings, so the first third couldn't jump the course, the middle third survived fairly well, and the last third didn't need to jump because they already had enough points. This mess of falls and no-shows really angered the crowd, so much that I thought we'd have a riot. The format has got to be fixed.

"Nicholas Alvarez de Boorques did an excellent job with the courses, though many, many people disagreed with me."

Sunday's two-round individual final courses were big, big jumps. The first group of horses had another big disadvantage—rain. Not only were these big fences, but the look was also spooky and the distance problems very difficult. There were only four clear rounds over this most taxing track, and one of them was Norman Dello Joio on Irish.

The second round, for the top 20 horses, was a monstrous and slightly static course. The double of oxers and the triple combination of vertical, oxer, oxer caused no end of disasters. The oxers were so wide that some horses gave up in mid-flight and let down before the back rail.

"To my mind the hero's hero was Norman Dello Joio."

Suspense was in the air when it came time for the four who'd been clear in the first round. The great gray, Milton, not only stumbled and had to pull out of a fence, but he also was not making the back rails of the oxers. He was out.

Dello Joio gave the ride of his life, just clipping off the front rail of a ramp oxer. Piet Raymakers jumped a fabulous clear on the careful mare Ratina Z but was a bit cautious on the turns and ended up with.25 time faults.

All the pressure was on Ludger Beerbaum and his brilliant mare Classic Touch. With the gold medal dangling before his eyes, he rode the course with the time uppermost in his mind, angling oxers and making sharp turns. I've never seen anything like it—with so much at stake he played with the course!

And so new heroes emerged—the German dressage team, Nicole Uphoff and Rembrandt, the Dutch jumping and dressage teams, and Ludger Beerbaum. But to my mind the hero's hero was Norman Dello Joio. Every horseman in the world realized what he and this green, green horse had done.

47

I Love Seeing Horses
All Around The World

December 1, 2000

Traveling the world is really fun (and educational too!). Traveling the world looking at horses is even more fun. And traveling the world and maybe buying a horse is the most fun of all.

Luckily for me, I had a grandmother who never stopped traveling. I was named for her late husband. And so being her "pet," I got to go along on lots of her trips. She also happened to be my sponsor as far as horses were concerned.

And so from this early background, traveling and horses have stayed with me my whole life as abiding passions. Actually, they've turned out to be quite compatible.

My first trip abroad was horse shopping for Larry Golding (Jay Golding's father) and the Laureling Farm. He sent me to France and England for 10 days. I came back empty-handed and told Larry we could find better at home. We bought a Thoroughbred from the legendary Benny O'Meara.

Otto Heuckeroth (although he was a German) and Bert de Nemethy (a Hungarian) insisted back in the '50s and '60s that we had the best horses in the world. We probably did. Look at the record books!

I'm probably prejudiced, but nothing beats a good old American Thoroughbred. These horses (that we don't see very often anymore) were big, light on their feet, elastic and powerful. They had heart and stamina and were quite sound. They had enormous scope and could jump any course in the world, including any Olympic Games.

The Europeans questioned our Thoroughbred's carefulness, and they might have been right. But if you found one with the scope and elasticity to jump clean, you couldn't beat him. He was faster.

Gem Twist epitomized the American Thoroughbred jumping horse. He won the best horse title at the 1990 World Equestrian Games. I think he might have been the greatest jumping horse of the century. He was certainly second to none.

Nowadays, due to the lack of availability of American Thoroughbreds, Americans are importing, breeding, and raising all kinds of horses. While those horses, in general, can't quite compete with what we used to have, they are certainly a usable substitute. In time, by crossing European sport horses with American Thoroughbreds, we might have quite a good horse indeed.

Canada also has good Thoroughbreds. They could be conformation hunter champions at the National Horse Show (N.Y.) or on the Canadian gold-medal team at the Olympics. Canadian Thoroughbreds were more often middleweight or heavyweight horses, bigger than ours and possessing more bone. They were a little coarser but could really jump. Now we can shop

261

in Canada and a see a lot of European crosses, especially horses of German extraction.

Argentina has historically been the greatest breeder and exporter of horses in Central or South America. The Argentinean Thoroughbred (of which the great Balbuco was a perfect example) is usually quite big and rangy and slightly more upside down. They're often volatile and a bit quirky in disposition. I haven't been to Brazil for many years to look at horses, but I intend to go this spring. They have many mixed breeds of jumpers, some small and wiry, and other horses of substance and power. My friends tell me Brazil is the place to go, but the horses are expensive.

Some years ago I went to Chile to shop. They had wonderful Thoroughbreds that were not only pretty but also of the most gorgeous color. Maybe it was the grass and hay. Usually the Chilean horse is small and, while a careful jumper, lacks power and scope for big grand prix events, but they have imported some warmbloods.

Alison Firestone's Jox and Vicky Roycroft's Apache exemplify the Australian Thoroughbred horse—usually very hot. The ones that have scope like Jox or Anne Kursinski's Eros are few and far between. But Australian Thoroughbreds as a group are quite careful jumpers. The best way to find horses in Australia or New Zealand is to go to their weekend shows and watch hundreds of younger ones.

On average, the New Zealand Thoroughbred is bigger and rangier than his Australian counterpart. They are race horses bred for a distance. That's one of the reasons their three-day event team has done so well. These horses often have rounder toplines than Australian Thoroughbreds, who can go a bit upside down. Again, there is a lot of European cross–breeding now in New Zealand, which should produce an interesting horse.

South Africa, like most of the English-speaking world, has always bred lovely Thoroughbred horses, quite a bit like ours. But it's a bit shut off from the rest of the world, so we don't get there much. And, due primarily to African horse sickness, until recently it was next to impossible to get horses out of South Africa.

Years ago the great place to shop in Europe was Ireland. The European dealers, especially the Italians, went to the Dublin Horse Show in droves. Now, however, Ireland has taken a bit of a back seat to the continent.

I think the Irish go too far away from the blood horse to predictably produce Olympic scope. What they do have, though, are lots of careful, honest, clever amateur-owner and junior jumpers, mostly of a half-bred type. The Irish horse is a real trier. He'll give you all he's physically got.

England and Scotland once relied on a breed or type to make a show jumper. Each horse was totally different—from a rangy Thoroughbred to a small Connemara pony. Many of the horses you now see in England and Scotland were imported as young horses from the continent. It's a good place to go look for horses because the horsemen are so very, very good.

Sweden has an enormous amount of horse breeding. Much of the stock was originally German. Sweden always had good jumpers. Many of them were chestnut with lots of white. They still have very pretty horses, but some can be spookier than I like.

To be honest, while I've ridden and shown in Denmark, I've never looked for horses there. People just don't think of going there. Being close to Holstein in northern Germany, many of the horses are basically the same breed and type. Don't forget Albert Voorn of Holland rode a Danish horse (Lando) to the silver medal at the Olympics this year.

Russia (and its ex-satellite countries) breeds tens of thousands of horses each year. And many of them must be able to jump. I always used to admire the hot Thoroughbreds of the old Soviet Union teams. They were so badly ridden, yet they still kept going.

There are many, many different breeds and types in Russia. It is one of the last frontiers for horse buying. But it's not an easy country to travel in, and now they say it can be quite dangerous.

Eastern Europe, namely Poland, Hungary, and the Czech Republic, is catching on now. They also have lots of horses of a German type. Whether it's the horse, the schooling, or both, I haven't seen a lot of horses with big scope come from there.

France has always provided some of the best horses in the world. In the old days, it was the Anglo-Arab, the Selle Francais and the French Thoroughbred. Now that Europe is an open continent, there seems to be a much broader mixture.

French horses, as a rule, are very honest and very careful. They will fight to the death. But one has to always look closely at their scope and soundness, and the French sometimes are difficult to deal with when it comes to buying their horses.

Belgium, being in the center of Europe, can be the best of all worlds. It seems all breeds and types of horses come through Belgium. I like their horses because they are often hot and have a lot of French blood, but they have the scope and power of a German horse. Unlike the French, the Belgians will usually sell anything at any time.

Holland and Germany are surely the most popular places for Americans to go today. The Dutch horse is usually capable, honest and steady, and the people are also a lot like the horses. The Dutch speak perfect English, and the lifestyle is not unlike ours. The Dutch horse is easier to ride, as a rule, than the German one. Perhaps it's because of the Irish mare in many of their pedigrees.

Germany breeds lots of horses; then the Germans market everything they do, and they have the very best.

If you can ride a good German horse, you'll have a lot of success. The good ones (usually with a quirky disposition) have tremendous scope and are careful. However, nine out of 10 German horses think "backwards." They lack natural impulsion. For most Americans, this doesn't work. We like to be carried, probably from our Thoroughbred heritage. We are sympathetic, but German horses need constant domination and discipline. Nobody will ride a German horse better than a German rider.

48

We Were So Close At The World Cup!

May 17, 2002

The venue for the FEI World Cup Final in Leipzig, Germany, was nothing short of vast. Five huge, rectangular shells surround an enormous glass, dome-like building in the center. From a practical point of view, this venue was excellent. It could house the competition arena and all the stabling, schooling rings, vendors, and offices for the management.

The main arena was huge and almost square in shape, much like the old Washington (D.C.) arena, but three or four times the size. There was no limit to what Frank Rothenberger, Europe's most popular course designer, could do—and did do—with the courses. And he did a super job, adding much-needed variety to every course. Some of our American designers could learn from that.

The Tuesday warm-up at this show allowed riders to spend 90 seconds in the arena to do what they wanted, much like our hunter warm-ups. It was clear at this point that the footing was going to be superb, with no slipping or sliding on the turns.

Wednesday is traditionally devoted to real classes for the second and third horses, classes that can also be used as warm-ups for the World Cup horses. This show offered a Table A (fastest clean round), a jump-off class, and a power-and-speed competition.

There were spectators on these weekdays, but not as many as we'd been led to believe would be there. The weekend was sold out, however, with a standing-room-only crowd that was most enthusiastic and, apparently, quite well informed. Having the final there was most important to the people of Leipzig, which used to be part of Communist East Germany, and they really appreciated it.

Thursday offered interesting young horses classes, as well as the World Cup's first leg. This class is run over a Table A-type course with Table C rules (converting each knockdown to 4 seconds).

This course again offered great variety, with a pen-like, skinny combination bordered by high pillars at fence 3AB, a massive liverpool oxer off a short turn, and an unusual spooky wall. There were three double combinations and five turns with short or long options.

I found the rather scopey, technical and careful course most interesting.

As a rule, the American team doesn't start off with a bang in the first leg, something they must learn to do. McLain Ward and Leslie Howard were our best finishers. The class was won by a very, very longshot, a young Polish boy named Jacek Zagor. He jumped clear and made every inside turn, riding an unbeatable round like it was a junior jumper class. It was undoubtedly Poland's biggest win since World War II.

267

Friday is the second leg, and again the course was excellent, offering lots of variety. It included two double combinations (oxer-vertical and triple bar-vertical), as well as a triple combination (vertical, oxer, oxer), a liverpool, and a skinny. This liverpool, like all the others, was filled to the brim with water, which makes a big difference to the horses.

Nine horses jumped clear, with Margie Engle being one of them. She made a marvelous comeback from the first night, when Perin didn't like the pen combination. McLain again went clean, which put him second behind the German superstar, Ludger Beerbaum.

The German team had qualified many more riders than any other country, and their strength was remarkable. By Friday evening they had four riders in the top six. This was no accident. As a country, they always work together and have a plan. They are most intelligent and aggressive, with a great work ethic. They breed tens of thousands of sport horses and have lots of young and talented riders. And, for me, it's nice to see how the Germans have softened their riding over the years and now ride forward, out of pace, more like we do.

The fences today are, for the most part, light rails, with bases and fill that take the horse's eye off the top rail. They are still very big jumps, although much more airy and careful than some years ago. The oxers are almost always absolutely square. A light, Thoroughbred-type horse with plenty of scope is the best for today's sport.

Saturday featured the grand prix, allowing horses not going in Sunday's last leg to have a consolation class, along with others not in the World Cup. This course was big too—high, wide, airy and square, made up almost entirely of bending lines. This class offered no luck for the Americans.

Sunday's final leg is a two-rounder. It ended up being the kind of course that seemed to ride a little easier than it looked.

It was quite a long course, with 14 numbered fences. Nevertheless, a few more than I'd anticipated jumped clear. McLain, Leslie and Ray Texel all jumped brilliantly clear rounds over this most formidable course, while Laura Kraut, Lauren Hough and Margie all put in excellent four-fault rounds. The Americans were coming to life, but for the most part it was too late in the game.

Ludger Beerbaum and his lovely chestnut mare Gladdys met an oxer a bit too deep and uncharacteristically dropped a rail. That left McLain in first, potentially the first American winner since Katharine Burdsall and The Natural won in Paris in 1987.

The last round was shorter but really big, really difficult, and really careful. You really needed a jumper and a rider.

Leslie and Priobert De Kalvarie were the only pair to jump a double-clear, which made them the winners of this leg—a tremendous accomplishment. She was the odds-on favorite to win this whole thing, but it just wasn't meant to be. Luck was just not on our side. We were so close!

McLain had a most unfortunate 12-fault round that left him tied for fourth with Leslie, behind Otto Becker, Ludger and Rodrigo Pessoa. This cannot diminish McLain's effort in anyone's eyes, however. I take my hat off to McLain's riding, to Lee McKeever's management, to owner Harry Gill, to supporter Sherry Robertson, and to all his family and staff. This team really knows how to play the game of international show jumping.

A DIFFERENT LOOK AND FEEL

"He did a super job, adding much-needed variety to the courses."

The countryside around Leipzig, which is in the former East Germany, about 80 miles southwest of Berlin, proved to be very flat farmland. I'd been teaching in Belgium, and as I drove on the new Autobahn to Leipzig with Chris Kappler and his fiancée, Jenny Bates, it certainly looked different than the western part of Germany.

(Chris and some other Americans had shown at Morsele, in Belgium, the weekend before as an indoor preparation for the World Cup. It was, I thought, a good strategy as we have so little opportunity to show indoors these days.)

Things were a bit plainer, simpler, and a bit drab, although not too bad. I'm sure in five or 10 years the whole of Germany will mesh and there will be few remnants of 45 years of Communist rule.

"The Americans were coming to life, but it was too late in the game."

One could almost depict the history of the ancient German town through its architecture. The really old buildings that had survived the tumult of the 20th century were really quite beautiful. Then you could see the Communist-style blocks of enormous and bleak slabs of concrete, which are really quite ugly. Then there were the new buildings, which were only a bit better. There is definitely a look and feel of the city that's quite different from the West.

The nicest thing about Leipzig proved to be its people. They couldn't have been nicer, friendlier or more helpful. And most spoke English.

And one can't visit Leipzig without seeing the railroad station. It's the biggest dead-end train station in Europe, perhaps the world. It's three stories high and houses arcades full of shops and restaurants.

49

What I Think Was Right
—And Wrong—About Athens

September 10, 2004

The Olympic organizing committees apparently now have a good recipe for Olympic equestrian venues—build it like they did in Atlanta (1996) and Sydney (2000), in a series of levels or tiers.

Like its two predecessors, in Athens the stable area was at the lowest point or level. And, by the way, these barns were permanently and beautifully built, spacious and airy.

The next level, sort of up a block, held the warm-up arenas. Athens had quite a few sand arenas and several good grass arenas. And the entrance to the cross-country course came directly out of the warm-up area.

But the top tier in Athens was quite different than Sydney or Atlanta: Two huge stadiums, one for dressage, with all-weather footing, and one for show jumping, with grass footing, along with two final warm-up rings.

Much of the jumping community was in Athens for the final show jumping day of the eventing. And we were mystified by the debacle that took place regarding the scoring of Bettina Hoy. It will always be a mystery to me.

How riders at this level and judges at this level could let a basic and flagrant violation of the rules unravel to this point is truly astounding. Luckily, after decisions were overturned right and left, the correct conclusion was drawn. And, unfortunately for the equestrians, this was after much wrangling by the lawyers.

I always enjoy the Olympics from a spectator's point of view. There is time to see everything, so I've watched the eventing and the dressage almost without exception since I first went to the Pan Am Games in Chicago in 1959.

Dressage judging is apparently more mysterious and perplexing even than the hunters and the equitation. The dressage community better get their house in order or they're going to kill the sport. Who would want to go to the time, trouble, heartache and expense to put up with the shenanigans I saw at these great Olympics?

Of course, the United States is not part of the European clique in dressage or show jumping. And we're certainly not a big part of the "old boys club" of the Federation Equestre Internationale. Still, transparency has to be part of the game.

But, back to show jumping. Olaf Petersen was the course builder and Leopoldo Palacios was the technical delegate. They're both masters of the sport.

Olaf's warm-up course (which doesn't count in the scoring) gave each rider 90 seconds to do his or her thing, and it proved typically bland and low. Olaf did present a rather spooky cutout wall and a stack of rails over open water. People could jump the wall several times if their horses didn't like it, and several did.

My strongest impression leaving the warm-up round was the excellent standard across the board of teams, horses, and riders.

My, how the average rider has improved! Most ride smoothly with their horses, in a beautiful position.

My first impression of the course for the first individual qualifying round was the colors of the fences—they very much reflected Mediterranean colors. Pastels, blues, beiges, oranges and lime greens. And they blended in so well to the background.

Yes, Olaf's course was technical and tricky enough, but it was the colors that added to the illusion, and his striding options that increased the difficulty. The very interesting and colorful wings on the sides of the fences were also distracting.

Olaf also presented a royal blue wall off the in-gate, nine strides to a pair of rust-colored oxers about 34 1/2 feet apart. This apparently was an optical problem, which appeared to be worse early in the day.

Again, the standard across the board was excellent. There were many powerful teams and individuals in Athens, and ours looked among the best.

The Nations Cup course on Tuesday was nothing short of magnificent. Again the colors of the fences and the construction of the wings were most unusual and impressive. Virtually every fence came down at one time or another.

Olaf's technical, bending-line incorporation of the open water was particularly memorable. Also challenging was the half-stride option of five or six strides from fence 3 to the double combination at fences 4A and B, and the oxer-vertical-oxer triple combination (fences 11ABC) before the five strides to the delicate plank.

One fence in particular caused concern from a judging point of view. The delicate plank at fence 12 kept blowing down in the relentless wind. Several horses were right on top of it when it blew down, causing one horse to jump a 3'6" fence and the other one to jump a two-foot fence. Neither, of course, was penalized.

Just as in Sydney four years ago, the footing proved to be a big problem. This relatively new turf had no root system, cupped out, and gave way as horses took off and landed. Three horses, including Chris Kappler's Royal Kaliber, broke down in the ring and had to be taken away in the horse ambulance.

I don't understand why footing is such a difficult thing to create, especially with all these footing specialists running around. It's a responsibility that officials from the FEI need to shoulder better.

For whatever reason, the footing appeared less of a problem in the second round, run under lights. They moved every fence over a couple of feet so the horses wouldn't be taking off and landing in the same places again, and they replaced the plank on top of fence 12 with a rail, even though the wind had disappeared.

The German team's triumph showed that, in every discipline, they are an example of ambition, unity, horsemanship and work ethic. They are true professionals in every sense of the word, and they're even nice. Of course, they have Ludger Beerbaum, whom I consider the greatest rider of the century, as their captain. He has such class and stature that he helps everyone else, not just his teammates.

Beezie Madden's double-clear rounds and Chris Kappler's clear and 4 faults helped secure the silver medal after an absolutely stupid jump-off against the Swedes. While the Germans were winning the competition, we were giving it away. We made too many mistakes, especially at the water, to have deserved gold.

Historically, some of the best riders have had "wateritis." We have to jump water more and learn how to school horses to jump it clean.

Yes, I'm very proud of our wonderful silver medal. But I keep thinking, "Close but no cigar!" There is more work to be done if we are ever to approach the pinnacle we reached in the 1980s.

[The U.S. team would eventually receive the gold medal when Beerbaum's horse was disqualified for a minor drug infraction, dropping the Germans to fourth.]

The individual final is run over two different courses, which are, of course, bigger than the Nations Cup. Some 45 riders qualified to start, all beginning anew with 0 faults.

Olaf's first round didn't appear as difficult as it proved to be. Again, almost every fence took its toll, especially both combinations. There were only two completely clear rounds.

Course B walked extremely difficult. The triple bar with five short strides to the vertical-vertical-oxer combination was the meat of the course, although, again, almost every fence came down at least once. And only two riders jumped clear.

When the dust settled, Cian O'Connor, a young but experienced Irish rider, won the gold with 4 faults. Rodrigo Pessoa and Chris Kappler had tied for silver with 8 faults and had to jump off, where Royal Kaliber went three-legged lame.

[After O'Connor's horse tested positive for two illegal drugs, Pessoa became the gold medalist and Kappler the silver medalist. Royal

276

Kaliber was humanely destroyed a month later as the result of his injury in Athens.]

This is the second Olympic Games in a row where I've lost great horses to treacherous footing. First it was Rhythmical in Sydney and now Royal Kaliber in Athens, both owned by the Kamine family. As we all know, it's hard enough to find such horses, let alone manage, school, and show them successfully.

First, I feel for the pain and discomfort the horses go through. Second, I feel for the heartache endured by all those involved with these wonderful horses.

I left these Olympic Games with an extremely bittersweet taste in my mouth. In fact, I am most discouraged with the powers that be. After all, it is the FEI's job to maintain the sport at this level. And these Olympic Games were certainly jinxed.

50

Las Vegas Hit A Home Run, Even If Our Riders Didn't

May 6, 2005

Although this was the third time Las Vegas had hosted the Budweiser FEI World Cup Show Jumping Final, it was the first time the Dressage World Cup Final came to town at the same time. Combining these two finals with the new and innovative hunter challenge, along with the live entertainment—singers, acrobats, Siegfried & Roy, and more—made a truly spectacular show.

If I were to rate this show, I'd give it an A+. It was, without a doubt, one of the most memorable horse events I've ever attended.

Part of all of our big shows must be a theatrical happening. So I must give special thanks to the Las Vegas Events Board of Trustees, Robert Ridland, John Quirk, and a host of other people who put the show on; the generosity of Budweiser and Offield Farm, plus the other great sponsors; and to Guilherme Jorge, who built such perfect and sensitive courses; and, yes, to Richard

Jeffery for his beautiful floral decor.

I always stay at the Bellagio, an easy 10-minute taxi ride to the show grounds, a fabulous complex called the Thomas & Mack Arena. I believe the stadium holds about 16,000 people, which is just right. The whole complex of stabling, tented warm-up arena, ramp and main ring couldn't be more convenient.

This is a small ring, not an easy place to build courses. But it proved even harder to house the dressage arena. Nonetheless, it all worked. And even on the Wednesday warm-up day, the seats were two-thirds full, especially for the dressage warm-up, where three horses used the square at once. The audiences were so, so educated. Like so many of us, they were interested in watching the horses school, like a mini-competition.

Guilherme's warm-up course consisted of eight fences: a bending line, a cutout wall, a liverpool, and a double combination.

Thursday I enjoyed watching the jumpers school on the flat, which I've always done since my teenage years at the National Horse Show in New York's Madison Square Garden. Of the foreigners, Ludger Beerbaum, Rodrigo Pessoa, Marcus Ehning and Hubert Bourdy stood out to me as far as position, simplicity and sensitivity were concerned. Most people today ride with an extremely long rein, which seems to be the fashion. It compromises control, and you don't see it with the dressage riders.

Our dressage riders were so great in Las Vegas. Debbie McDonald and Brentina are one together, a perfect partnership. And I've never seen Robert Dover and Kennedy go better or more consistently. Leslie Morse and Guenter Seidel are also great entries. The judging and the scores were more comprehensible in Las Vegas than at the Athens Olympics last summer.

279

Staging both of these finals together is a brilliant concept and must be done more often. It made for a unique event. It was an indoor show of a similar atmosphere to the old Madison Square Garden.

The first leg of the jumping final is run over a Table A course under Table C rules. There is a height restriction of 1.50 meters (4'10"), so it doesn't appear very big. Guilherme very cleverly asked the most difficult forward questions on the first part of the course to catch the horses that were over-trained. There were striding options, turning options, and a great variety of fences. It finished with a careful triple combination.

Yet again the Europeans attacked this first leg and rode on the offensive. We appeared intimidated and rode on the defensive, often tentative and weak, with the exception of Kim Frey on Marlou. I was most disappointed this first night.

Now, to give our team some excuses (which I don't like doing!), we don't show much anymore indoors. And our professionals' horse lifestyles are so different than the Europeans, who just concentrate on the international game. But that must be a different article in the future.

Friday night was the second leg of the Show Jumping World Cup, one round with a jump-off against the clock, at night.

The jump-off course featured striding options (just off!), a bending line to a combination, shorter rails, and a tough last line. This was a tall vertical, then 49' 8" to a tall, delicate gate, then 45' 6" to an oxer. This took rideability to lengthen and shorten their strides!

Perhaps this course could have been a touch bigger, but Guilherme got the result he wanted with nine clear rounds.

We didn't have a great night the second leg. The Europeans are riding beautifully—softly and smoothly—and their style in general has also vastly improved over the years. Meredith Michaels-Beerbaum and Shutterfly were particularly impressive as they took over the lead.

On Saturday we started to get going (better late than never!) and had five clean in the Las Vegas Grand Prix. By the way, this too was an excellent course. Anne Kursinski ended up second with Roxana and Candice King finished third with Coco Cabana. Schuyler Riley and Richard Spooner followed them. Actually, we had a great class.

I have rarely witnessed dressage on such a standard as we saw here in Las Vegas in the freestyle final—to a completely packed house. The top tests in particular will be etched in my mind for a long time. And what audience appreciation, reaction and participation.

We had something very innovative and interesting in Las Vegas called the AHJF Hunter Challenge. Two teams—one European (Michael Whitaker, Nick Skelton, Rodrigo Pessoa and Marcus Ehning) and one American (Louise Serio, Scott Stewart, John French and Peter Pletcher)—went head-to-head over two courses, one of which was to be ridden as a handy hunter class.

First, let me say all the horses were lovely. And second, all the riders rode well. As a group, the Europeans not only rode more offensively (yet again!), but they also looked "tighter" doing

"It was, without a doubt, one of the most memorable horse events I've ever attended."

"I have rarely witnessed dressage on such a standard as we saw here in Las Vegas."

281

it. We've gotten a bit soft, slack and sloppy. It's another reason I'm afraid we all left Las Vegas with our tails a bit between our legs.

Sunday's finale is a two-round competition, over two different courses, and somewhat bigger. Both of these courses proved to be about perfect and asked literally every question as far as variety of fence and type of combination. I cannot praise this course builder enough.

Meredith won brilliantly as Michael Whitaker ended up reserve. For our team, we have to applaud Kim Frey and Schuyler Riley, who did beautifully.

Yes, Las Vegas hit a home run with the bases loaded. From this perspective, I'm proud of our country. But from the competitive point of view, there is a lot of work to be done. We just have to pull ourselves up by the bootstraps, get working, and do what we all know how to do, but even better.

Still to come in the "Chronicle Comment Series":

John Strassburger: *The Things I Think Really Matter*
(March 2007)

Victor Hugo-Vidal: *Trips Of A Lifetime*
(May 2007)

Denny Emerson: *The Event Horse Is Truly Special*
(November 2007)

Anne Gribbons: *Inside And Outside The Letters*
(March 2008)

Made in the USA
Lexington, KY
18 September 2010